SOCIAL
PROGRAM
EVALUATION

F. E. Peacock Publishers, Inc.
Itasca, Illinois

SOCIAL PROGRAM EVALUATION

Guidelines for Health, Education, and Welfare Administrators

Tony Tripodi
Phillip Fellin
Irwin Epstein
THE UNIVERSITY OF MICHIGAN

TO FEDELE F. FAURI

Vice-President for
State Relations and Planning

The University of Michigan

CONTENTS

5 USE OF CONSULTATION   113

ACKNOWLEDGMENTS

This book is the result of a truly collaborative process among the authors. Our ideas were influenced by personal interactions with faculty colleagues, students, and administrators and evaluators of social programs. In particular, many of our thoughts about social program evaluation were stimulated by associations with Richard A. Cloward, Amitai Etzioni, David Fanshel, Samuel Finestone, and Alfred J. Kahn, Columbia University; James Bieri, University of Texas; Edgar Borgatta and Sheldon Rose, University of Wisconsin, Madison; Fred P. DelliQuadri, University of Wisconsin, Milwaukee; David French, Brandeis University; and our present colleagues at the University of Michigan, Louis Ferman, Roger Lind, Eugene Litwak, Henry J. Meyer, and Richard B. Stuart. Moreover, we have been especially stimulated by the writings of A. Etzioni, D. T. Campbell, R. A. Cloward, G. W. Fairweather, D. Fanshel, L. Ferman, E. Herzog, H. H. Hyman, A. J. Kahn, O. Klineberg, A. S. Levine, S. Levitan, H. Stein, E. A. Suchman, and C. R. Wright.

We are grateful to the administration of The University of Michigan School of Social Work for providing us the intellectual climate necessary to complete our work. In this respect, we are particularly thankful to Fedele F. Fauri and Robert D. Vinter.

We express our deepest appreciation to the following members of the secretarial staff who helped prepare portions of the manuscript: Carla Barnes, Carol Mutton, Linda Wik, and Daneen Woolson; and we acknowledge the special contribution of Barbara Hiebbner who typed the final draft of the manuscript.

Graduate students who gave us invaluable assistance in locating references on evaluation and in preparing an index for the manuscript were Betty Bachman, Fran Kaplan, and Carol MacMurray.

We thank F. E. Peacock, our publisher, and his associates, Thomas LaMarre and Joyce Usher, for their helpful advice and efficient services.

Finally, we are appreciative for the encouragement of our wives, Roni Tripodi, Phyllis Fellin, and Lyn Epstein, and the children in our families: Anthony, Lee Anna, Rachel, and David; Annette, Campion, Cecilia, Christopher, and Mary; and Daniel and Rebecca.

Chapter One

AN INTRODUCTION

THE DEMAND FOR EVALUATION

In recent years, administrators and program planners have given considerable attention to the modification of existing health, education, and welfare programs and to the development of new programs to meet the needs of selected segments of the population. These modifications and developments are often based on the assumption that traditional programs have not been satisfactory in delivering needed services or in promoting social change.

As the search for innovation and relevance in program planning and development has increased, demands for evaluation have also increased. Program directors are being asked by funding sources, professional groups, clientele, and a more sophisticated general public to demonstrate not only the needs to which their programs are addressed, but also the contributions that they make in solving or alleviating social problems. In addition, questions about the management of funds and the relative costs and efficiency of alternative programs are constantly being raised. For the administrator, the availability, appropriateness and adequacy of program evaluation can determine the success and/or survival of a program.

Despite the increasing demand for evaluation from outside sources, administrators are often skeptical about the merits of program evaluation. Frequently they are confused by the claims and counter claims of evaluation consultants representing different schools of organizational analysis. Moreover, some program directors view evaluation cynically, as simply a device which is used by agency supporters to justify current operations. Alternatively, in the hands of program critics, evaluation is viewed as a justification for reductions in program funding. In addition, legislators and clients alike have questioned the costs of evaluation—the former in terms of the lack of success in providing significant feedback of information to programs, and the latter in terms of the direct services that these funds might otherwise provide.

THE PURPOSE OF THIS BOOK

Although administrators are frequently perplexed by decision-making problems concerning evaluation, most books on evaluation are written for evaluators.[1] These are concerned with logical and practical procedures in the conduct of evaluation studies. Often they include sections pertaining to the administrative context in which evaluation takes place, and discussions of potential barriers to evaluation which emanate from conflict between program and evaluation personnel. But, typically, little attention is devoted to the problems of administrators or program directors in deciding when and what kind of evaluation is needed and how to utilize the results for making programmatic decisions. Consequently, the administrator who searches the literature is likely to find that it is of little use to him in making the kinds of evaluation decisions he has to make.

This book is written primarily for practicing administrators and program directors in the fields of health, education, and welfare. In addition, it may be used as a supplementary text by students of administration, program development, evaluation, and research in such fields as social work, public health, education, public administration, and sociology.[2]

Our basic purposes are to provide a framework for making decisions about social program evaluations and to increase the sensitivity of program directors to differ-

---

[1] See Chapter Four for references on the conduct of evaluation, particularly those included in the section on social research techniques.

[2] A number of the ideas presented in this book are extensions and modifications of the following article by Tony Tripodi, Irwin Epstein, and Carol MacMurray: "Dilemmas in Evaluation: Implications for Administrators of Social Action Programs", *American Journal of Orthopsychiatry*, October, 1970, pp. 850–857.

ent issues in evaluation. More specifically, our aim is to present guidelines which can be used by program directors so that they can be more knowledgeable about initiating and sustaining evaluation studies and can make the best use of evaluation consultants.

Directors of health, education, and welfare programs are committed to improving societal conditions through their programs. Accordingly, they have important and difficult responsibilities to maintain. They are accountable to significant and diverse community groups, and, more specifically, they are responsible for reporting on program operations and achievements to intended program beneficiaries, program sponsors, program staff, and the general public.

In addition to their many responsibilities, social program administrators must frequently contend with pressures from a variety of sources. In many instances, they must make quick decisions in ambiguous situations and with little systematic information for guidance. Although it is not possible for all decisions to be made on strictly rational grounds, we assume that program directors prefer to base decisions about their programs on available, objective information in order to provide the most effective and efficient services possible within the scope of their programs. Moreover, with increasing demands for evaluation, program directors are not always in a position to make decisions about whether or not an evaluation should be conducted. Often, evaluations are demanded by funding agencies or by pressure groups outside of the program. But even in those situations, the program director is in a position to influence the conduct and utilization of an evaluation. The more sophistication the program director has about evaluation, the more likely it is that he can play a role in increasing the relevance of an evaluation of his program. Furthermore, the program director is often the primary consumer of evaluation studies; and, as an effective administrator, he *should* play a major role in planning evaluations of his program.

There are substantive differences among health, education, and welfare programs, but there are also many similarities involved in the administration and an evaluation of such programs. Consequently, we attempt to stress similar problems of evaluation for these different types of social programs. A major emphasis is on differential evaluation, i.e., different kinds of evaluation questions and techniques geared to different stages of program development. But the central thesis of this book is that evaluation is a management technique for the systematic feedback of information to be used to improve social programs.

SOCIAL PROGRAMS AND SOCIAL PROGRAM EVALUATION

Social Programs

Social programs are conceived broadly as having the goals of providing health, education, or welfare services for the advancement of individual or social change. Programs vary in such dimensions as the range and complexity of objectives, staff size and diversity, administrative structure, length of time in operation, operating expenditures, sources of support, and physical location. One program may include the entire range of objectives within a particular agency, such as the Office of Economic Opportunity's community action programs. Another program might include only a limited segment of an agency's activities, such as the use of non-professionals as public-health aides in a neighborhood health clinic. Established programs as well as developing programs are considered to be social programs. Thus, all of the following may be considered social programs: the total operations of a public welfare department; the activities of a welfare-rights organization; an effort to deliver chest x-ray services to a rural poor group; inoculation programs for influenza; reading tutorials; and the entire activities of a public school system.

Although the content of social programs and the means for achieving their goals may be different, all programs have similar problems to solve. Among these problems are location of resources, allocation of funds, maintenance of operating budgets, reporting to interested groups, and the justification of decisions regarding program planning and development. Moreover, social programs go through roughly similar stages in the process of program development.

Stages of Program Development

Program development may be described as a process with three sequential and interrelated stages: program initiation, program contact, and program implementation.[3] *Program initiation* refers to that stage in which the ideas for a program are translated into a plan of action, and in which necessary resources are secured. It involves all of the planning and preparations required before the content of the program can be delivered to its recipients. In this initial stage of development, program directors are concerned primarily with the procurement or selection of material resources, staff, technology and clientele.

Program contact is that stage in which a program has achieved its objectives of initiation, and is devoting its efforts to the active engagement of a target population with the program staff. The program focuses on providing relevant program content to its designated clientele. In this stage of development, program directors are concerned with locating physical, social and psychological obstacles to the effective delivery of services; locating other community resources which will aid, or impede, or substitute for the program's own activities; and so forth.

---

[3] A similar conception of program development can be found in *Social Change in Complex Organizations,* by Jerald Hage and Michael Aiken, Random House, Inc., New York, 1970.

Program implementation is that stage in which a program, having achieved the necessary conditions of initiation and program contact, applies its technology, services, etc. toward the attainment of ultimate program goals. Here, the program director is concerned with the extent to which major organizational goals are achieved. In this stage, criteria for follow-up activities and possible program termination are specified.

We recognize that these stages overlap somewhat, but they will be useful for specifying the conditions necessary for successful operation at different points in program development. In Chapter Two we will examine program development in detail, and illustrate program requisites within the different stages of development for a variety of health, education, and welfare programs. Moreover, in that chapter we will provide guidelines so that a program director can determine in which stage of development his program is.

Social Program Evaluation

Planning for social program evaluation depends to a great extent on specifying program requisites within the different stages of development. This is necessary so that both evaluators and consumers of evaluation know what is to be evaluated. In addition to the delineation of program requisites and goals, there likewise must be a clear specification of the proposed evaluation and its objectives. Program administrators and professional evaluators may have different conceptions of evaluation, and the failure to articulate such differences may result in inadequate planning for evaluation studies. For example, some differences appear to arise from varying uses of the word "scientific." What is scientific, objective, and value-free for one person may be non-scientific, subjective, and value-laden for another. Among evaluators, for example, Suchman[4] uses "scientific" to refer to the incorporation of experimental and control groups in evaluative research; Hayes[5] discusses the art of evaluation and implies that "scientific" refers to the obtaining of objective, systematic, and comprehensive evidence related to program activities; and Sherwood[6] broadens the definition of evaluation to include strategies and skills other than those of social research.

Another potential source of variation in conceptions of evaluation pertains to differing emphases on one or more of the following dimensions of evaluation: program efforts, program effectiveness, and program efficiency. Evaluation of *program efforts* refers to the description of the type and quantity of program activities. Evaluation of *program effectiveness* is concerned with whether or not intended outcomes, and beneficial un-

---

[4] Suchman, Edward A., *Evaluative Research: Principles and Practice in Public Service and Social Action Programs,* Russell Sage Foundation, New York, New York, 1967.

[5] Hayes, Samuel P., Jr., *Evaluating Development Projects,* UNESCO, Second Edition, reprinted, Belgium, 1967.

[6] Sherwood, Clarence C., "Issues in Measuring Results of Social Action Programs," *Welfare in Review,* Vol. 5, No. 7, 1967, pp. 13–17.

intended consequences, have been attained as a result of program efforts; and evaluation of *program efficiency* is devoted to determining the relative cost of achieving these outcomes.

Throughout the book, we regard social program evaluation as a device for the feedback of program information to program directors and to other persons responsible for the continual development of social programs. More precisely, *social program evaluation is the systematic accumulation of facts for providing information about the achievement of program requisites and goals relative to efforts, effectiveness, and efficiency within any stage of program development. The facts of evaluation may be obtained through a variety of relatively systematic techniques, and they are incorporated into some designated system of values for making decisions about social programs.*

Basic to our conception of social program evaluation is the idea of differential evaluation. *Differential evaluation* is a process of asking different evaluation questions of program efforts, effectiveness, and efficiency for each program stage of development, and then choosing those evaluation techniques which are most appropriate to the evaluation objectives. In Chapter Three we will present a range of different kinds of evaluation objectives for health, education, and welfare programs; and, in Chapter Four, selected evaluation techniques will be presented and discussed in order to provide the administrator with some information about their use. Included among them are *monitoring techniques,* such as the administrative audit and accountability audits, *cost-analytic techniques,* and *social-research techniques.*

Throughout this book we will emphasize that evaluation is not synonymous with formalized research techniques, and that different evaluation techniques are more or less appropriate for providing information to accomplish different evaluation objectives. Thus, the administrative audit may be most appropriate for evaluating program efforts during the program initiation stage, while a combination of experimental and survey methods may be most appropriate for evaluating program effectiveness during program implementation.

Social-program evaluation provides facts relevant to a determination of the achievement of program goals, but these facts may be interpreted differently. Although there are varying degrees of objectivity in the compilation of facts for an evaluation, the conduct and interpretation of evaluations is imbedded in a set of values regarding program goals and the "social good." Essentially, a *value* is a stated opinion of what is or is not desirable, and it is possible that individual values and societal values may be discrepant. For example, a program devoted to increasing the occupational skills of high school students may cause program participants to drop out of school in order to obtain a job. Those drop-outs may be regarded as failures by school authorities, but as successes by the program staff.

Another example pertains to welfare recipients. On the one hand, welfare mothers who receive welfare payments may be regarded by some persons as failures

if they receive those payments for more than a stipu-
lated period of time. On the other hand, it might be
argued that those welfare mothers may be providing
necessary care and supervision for their children, and
if they do this well the program might be construed as
successful. In a public-health program which involves
the dissemination of birth control devices, a reduction
in the birth rate for a particular ethnic group may be
regarded as desirable by some persons, while the intended "beneficiaries" may view the reduction of their
birth rate as undesirable since it may be regarded as
an attempt to lower their dignity and self-respect.
Hence, the same facts, irrespective of the objectivity
maintained in securing them, could be construed as indicative of program success or failure.

PROGRAM DIRECTORS AND EVALUATION

Pressures on Program Directors

There are various kinds of pressures on social program directors for evaluation. There may be *mandatory*
evaluations requested by funding groups, boards of
directors, or higher administrative authorities. These
evaluation requests may take such forms as progress
reports on the accomplishments and failures of the
program, reports which demonstrate that the program
management is responsible regarding its accounting
procedures and its allocations of funds, and so forth.

The program director must comply with those requests, for they are from groups to which he is directly accountable. If he does not respond to such requests, he may either argue that an evaluation is not needed or he may risk the possibility of not receiving continued support for his program. Particularly with developing programs which may be funded for a short period of time by such sponsors as the federal government, the program director may be caught in a conflict between program needs and the pressure for evaluation from the funding agency. In addition to these pressures, there may be few funds available for the conduct of evaluation, and the group that requests evaluation may not know, itself, what information it wants. Thus, the program director may be confronted with the dilemma of deciding what kind of evaluation, at what cost, is sufficient.

Some mandatory evaluations are conducted and funded by persons not directly involved with the social programs. In those instances, the program director may believe that he is one of the objects of evaluation, and fear that his job is in jeopardy. Hence, he may be reluctant to participate in the evaluation, and suspicious of the evaluation effort.

Pressures for evaluation may also arise from *social and political groups* which may be directly or indirectly involved with the social program. Charges regarding alleged discriminatory practices, program inequities, and mismanagement of funds may be made, with the possible result that an investigation of program practices is initiated. Difficult or impossible demands may be made on a program director, yet his competence is brought into question if he is unable to respond with factual information that he has accumulated about the program. Thus, external demands may compel the program director to call for an internal evaluation, i.e., self evaluation, of his program.

The pressure for *internal evaluation* may arise from the program director and his staff, with the primary purpose of improving the program. For example, there may be a perceived lack of success of the program, or it might be felt that there should be some reallocation of program activities. On the other hand, the pressures may arise from the professions to which the program administration and staff belong; they may believe that they are obligated to provide a quantity and quality of service that is in keeping with current professional standards.

The Role of the Program Director

Due to a variety of pressures, and perhaps to skepticism regarding the purposes of evaluation, program directors may believe that they have minor roles to play in the planning of evaluation. Program directors are often preoccupied with finding ways to get the most from their budgets, trying to obtain resources for improving the operations of the program, and attempting to keep good financial records. At the same time, program directors must be aware of the activities of the personnel who are operating the program, and keep up with their public-relations and public-information obligations. When a mandatory evaluation is called for, a program director may be reluctant to devote much staff time and energy to it. He may not want to divert funds from maintaining program operations to the evaluation, and he may even view evaluation as a device which could be used only for the purpose of justifying cuts in the program's operating expenses.

In spite of the above difficulties, program directors can play a key role in the planning of social program evaluations. Indeed, if the notion of evaluation as a management tool is accepted, then program directors have a primary responsibility to plan for evaluations of their programs. Furthermore, from a practical point of view, the more the program director knows about his program from evaluation, the more able he is to improve the program and to respond to the demands for evaluation from groups to which he is accountable.

A program director does not need to be an expert in conducting program evaluations in order to participate meaningfully in planning for program evaluation. But what does a program director need to know in order to contribute to the process of planning for an evaluation? He should have some conception of different kinds of evaluation and the dilemmas of evaluation with which he is confronted, and he should have sufficient skills to know when to use evaluation consultants for evaluating different stages of program development. In connection with the above, we will specify in Chapter Five the major dilemmas of evaluation which confront administrators of social programs: evaluation at what cost, what kind of evaluation, evaluation by whom, and evaluation for whom. In addition, several guidelines which might be useful in making decisions to resolve those dilemmas are presented. Moreover, in Chapter Four, we will indicate possible expectations of evaluation consultants who are expert in each of the techniques presented; and in Chapter Five, we will specify ways in which the program director can use evaluation consultants more effectively.

THE SOCIO-POLITICAL CONTEXT OF EVALUATION

Social Relationships in Evaluation

The process of evaluation involves obtaining systematic information within a context of social relationships.[7] Persons who have vested interests in the planning and the results of an evaluation may represent different ideologies and value systems. Therefore, a crucial element in obtaining useful evaluations is the extent to which the key persons involved in evaluation

---

[7] Many of the ideas in this section were derived from the article by Louis A. Ferman, "Some Perspectives on Evaluating Social Welfare Programs," *The Annals of the American Academy of Political and Social Science*, Vol. 385, September, 1969, pp. 143–156.

are able to make appropriate accommodations to each other. Thus, useful evaluations are more likely to occur when these conditions are met:

1. There is a clarification of the purposes of the evaluation among the key persons involved.
2. There is an agreed-upon commitment, contractual or understood, regarding the uses and possible consequences of the evaluation.

The key persons who may participate in the planning and the utilization of evaluation studies are the evaluator and his staff, the program director and his staff, persons with fiduciary responsibility for the program (such as sponsors and higher level management), and potential consumers who have no direct fiduciary or operating responsibilities regarding the program. Of course, the persons who participate in evaluation vary from program to program, and the number and diversity of persons involved depend upon such factors as the size and complexity of the program being evaluated.

Evaluations are initiated most frequently by program sponsors, separate from or in conjunction with program management. Typically, an evaluation consultant is sought, and the planning for evaluation is done by the consultant, who elicits cooperation from program administration and staff. In the conduct of an evaluation there is interaction primarily among the evaluation staff, program staff, and program administration. The key persons who participate in the utilization of results are those closest to the decision-making power, i.e., the program sponsors and administration.

Interests of the primary groups who participate in evaluation vary. The evaluator may be concerned with the generalization of his findings to other programs and with the production of a piece of work which is respectable to his professional colleagues. Program staff is most interested in rendering services to its clientele, and may view evaluation as an encroachment on staff time; while program sponsors may be most interested in program expenditures and efficiency. With the cooperation of these groups in the planning for evaluation, the results of evaluation are more likely to be understood and used.

The Political Process in Evaluation

In a study which reviewed five different planning efforts in community health, Conant[8] concluded that the major constraints on community-health planning are political. Referring to "political" as the conflict between power groups, he points out that planners must deal with interest-group pressures and counter pressures that arise in negotiations necessary for implementing a plan.

Since evaluations provide information that can be

[8] Conant, Ralph W., *The Politics of Community Health,* National Commission on Community Health Services, Public Affairs Press, Washington, D.C. 1968.

used for planning, it is not surprising that evaluations are also influenced by political considerations. Thus, for example, the Westinghouse evaluation of Head Start programs in 1969 became controversial because it did not produce convincing evidence that Head Start programs were effective, after they had been endorsed by a variety of interest groups as the most popular of the O.E.O. programs.[9]

Some programs are opposed, or heartily endorsed, irrespective of program accomplishments. In addition to Head Start, there are other programs which represent interests of different pressure groups: breakfast programs by the Black Panthers; summer recreation programs intended to keep people off the streets so they won't riot; job-training programs; and so forth. Such programs are often influenced by political decisions and compromises. They may be pet projects of influential groups, political tradeoffs, or token efforts to indicate that there is interest in certain groups. Evaluations of programs like those above are influenced by the political process, and may be encouraged or discouraged as a result of the relative power positions of those for or against the programs.

Just as political realities are necessary considerations in the planning of social programs, they are also important in evaluation. Program directors must engage

---

[9] Williams, Walter, and Evans, John W., "The Politics of Evaluation: The Case of Head Start," *The Annals of the American Academy of Political and Social Science*, Vol. 385, September, 1969, pp. 118–132.

in the process of negotiation and change among relevant pressure groups in the operation of their programs. Program directors usually are more skilled than evaluators in working within the political processes that directly involve their programs. Therefore, their skills should be included in the planning of an evaluation. Naive evaluators without political sophistication may draw up evaluation plans that are irrelevant and unrealistic for decision makers. This is why we advocate clarity in negotiations among program staff, evaluators, and other principal interest groups prior to the conduct of an evaluation.

THE POTENTIAL OF EVALUATION

Differential evaluation can provide useful information about social programs. This result is most probable when the socio-political climate is conducive to honest inquiry so that there is a commitment to the use of evaluation as a management tool for expanding knowledge and making decisions about social programs. An obvious precondition for evaluation, then, is a state of uncertainty about the social program and the felt need to reduce that uncertainty. Although evaluation studies do not produce *absolutely certain* information about the achievement of program objectives, they can provide relatively objective data which reduce the amount of uncertainty about program achievements. The knowledge derived from evaluation studies ranges in its degree of relative certainty—from hypotheses and simple facts to verified hypotheses which can be generalized to a variety of situations. This information can be used for program planning, staff development, and the reporting of program assets and liabilities to various groups to which the program is accountable.

By contrast, evaluation is least likely to provide useful information for developing and modifying social programs in situations such as the following:

1. Evaluation is used as a last resort by administrators to force staff consistency, and there is little interest in accumulating systematic information other than the monitoring of staff efforts.
2. Evaluation is used solely as a device for compiling information about the incompetence of selected individuals with the general purpose of discrediting those individuals.
3. Evaluation is used as a device selectively to collect *only* information which supports or undermines a social program.

In our view, abuses of evaluation such as those listed above lead to skepticism and cynicism concerning evaluation studies. In the chapters which follow, we will provide a framework for program directors so that they can plan for useful evaluations. Toward this end, our purpose is to increase the potential of evaluation with the hope that the results of evaluation studies will be utilized more effectively.

Chapter Two

PROGRAM DEVELOPMENT

In the previous chapter, the idea was introduced that social programs move through similar stages of development—program initiation, program contact, and program implementation. Moreover, it was suggested that the current stage of a program, or the stage to which it is attempting to move, will determine which of a wide range of evaluation objectives and evaluation techniques should be applied to it. This matching of evaluation objectives and techniques to a stage of program development was called "differential evaluation." In this chapter, the notion of program development is described in greater detail as it applies to specific health, education, and welfare programs. Then some guidelines are offered for identifying program stages. The relation between program stage and evaluation will be taken up in the following chapter.

STAGES OF PROGRAM DEVELOPMENT

Health, education, and welfare programs vary in a great many ways. Aside from the obvious substantive differences, programs vary in the degree to which they are committed to single versus multiple goals. In the field of education, for example, a tutorial program may be designed for the single purpose of increasing reading ability in a given population. By contrast, Project Head Start was designed to achieve multiple purposes, e.g., increasing low-income children's psychological readiness for school; increasing low-income parents' participation in and concern about their children's education; providing health examinations and treatment, etc. Likewise, health programs may be set up simply to provide chest x-rays or vaccinations on the one hand, or to provide comprehensive medical care for people on the other.

Programs also vary in the complexity of their technologies. A food-stamp program, for example, does not rely on the manipulation of a highly complex technology to achieve its goals. Here the problem is often simply one of dissemination of information and of the stamps themselves. Alternatively, a psychiatric clinic makes use of highly complex techniques for selecting, diagnosing, treating, and discharging its clientele.

Other bases of program variation are size, longevity, degree of centralization, type of physical plant and location, etc. Despite these differences, however, all social programs must solve similar developmental problems. They must first be able to secure sufficient material, social and technological resources to initiate a program. Second, they must make contact with their designated clientele. Third, they must effectively supply a service or apply a technology, or both, to their individual, group, or organizational clientele.

Before a discussion of program stages in greater detail, some qualifiers are in order. First, neither the complexity of program goals and/or technology, nor the length of time a program has been in existence is necessarily an indication of more "advanced" stages of program development. Thus, for example, a highly complex open-heart surgery program and facility may never transcend the problem of recruitment, training and maintenance of staff sufficiently skilled to implement the program. Family-service agencies, as another example, may have great longevity and equally great difficulty in effectively engaging low-income clientele. The causes of such failure in program contact may be many. However, the essential point is that longevity and complexity are not indicative of the stage of program development.

A second important point is that different programs within the same agency may be in different stages of development. A public school may be effectively implementing an educational program for "normal" youngsters at the same time that it is attempting to initiate a special-education program for the orthopedically handicapped. Each of these programs requires evaluation in terms of its own stage of development.

Third, it is important to note that not all programs simply progress linearly from one stage to another through time. All stages can present problems that are likely to persist to one degree or another. A public welfare agency, for example, must simultaneously handle the problems of staff recruitment and training, client contact and service implementation. Some programs progress in a kind of spiral pattern. A welfare-rights organization may recruit workers to organize welfare recipients to secure more services which will in turn be used as a resource for recruitment of new members, etc. In each of the above situations, judgments must be made about which stage of development is dominant, or which stage offers the greatest difficulty.

Fourth, some programs may be concerned entirely and appropriately with their success in making contact with their clientele. This is true when the implementation of program content has already proved to be effective in achieving ultimate program goals. Thus, for example, administrators of a program to bring food to starving children in underdeveloped areas may not wish to evaluate the effects of milk and other foodstuffs on the physical health of recipients. More likely they will be interested in measuring the extent to which food reaches its designated clientele instead of going into the local black market.

Despite the foregoing qualifications, almost all social

programs are involved in solving sequentially the problems of program initiation, contact, and implementation; and a program must effectively deal with each of these stages before it can move on to the next. The unique problems and characteristics of each stage and their relationship to health, education, and welfare programs will be explored in some detail.

PROGRAM INITIATION

Program initiation is the first stage of program development. It is during this stage that necessary material, social and technological resources are secured. Although initiation activities vary from program to program, all social programs must deal with the problems of procuring or developing competent staff, financial and physical resources, and social legitimation. Also included in this stage is the planning process: determining a need for the program; specifying program objectives and appropriate technologies for reaching these objectives; identifying a target client population of individuals or organizations and establishing eligibility criteria; spelling out staff functions, personnel policies and practices, and so forth.

These activities represent a necessary part of initiating any social program. Some specific examples of program initiation problems in health, education, and welfare programs are presented below.

Examples of Program Initiation

Health: A community-based public-health organization decides to try to educate the surrounding community regarding the advantages of fluoridation as a means of reducing tooth decay. The organization may undertake a survey of the attitudes of the general public on this issue. If a need for such a program of education is established, a competent staff will have to be recruited to bring the issue to the community. Decisions about the most effective strategies for involving the community, the techniques for neutralizing the arguments of groups opposed to such a plan, etc., will have to be made. In addition, staff are likely to be involved in locating or developing appropriate source materials to use in bringing their message to the public. Offices, telephones and meeting places will be required. Moreover, legitimation of the program by local professionals or professional associations may be necessary.

Education: An Upward Bound program is proposed for a particular secondary school in a low-income area. The purpose of the program is to identify low-income children who have the intellectual potential for college but lack the necessary economic and social resources. Program initiation in this case involves decisions about the bases for determination of eligibility; the utilization of existing secondary-school staff, or the hiring of new staff to administer the program; the procurement of material resources for economic support of college-bound youngsters; and so forth. Program strategies will have to be developed to change the attitudes of youngsters who might not ordinarily anticipate going to college. In addition, remedial programming in reading comprehension and written expression is likely to be needed. Thus, before the first potential client is contacted, the program administrator must establish the necessary conditions and make the necessary decisions for initiating the program.

Welfare: A public welfare agency is required to institute a work-incentive program (WIN) for public-welfare recipients. Since the federal government will be providing the financial resources, the problems of initiation will more likely be related to development of criteria for eligibility for the program, and decisions about the kinds of job-training programs which will have to be developed. In addition, a major effort toward procurement of employment opportunities will have to be made. For all of these decision-making tasks and their implementation, a competent staff will have to be selected. Career lines would have to be developed for these workers as well as for their clients.

PROGRAM CONTACT

Program contact is the second stage of program development. After the objectives of the program initiation stage are accomplished, contact must be made with potential program beneficiaries. Efforts to contact potential clients may involve mass-media advertisements, door-to-door canvassing, a word-of-mouth campaign, flyers in mailboxes, contacts with personnel in other agencies who may be sources of referral, and so forth.

Direct contact may take place in different locations. Some agencies employ "outreach" programs which bring the program to the homes in the client community. Other programs make use of intermediary facilities such as "bloodmobiles" which are moveable, but which require equipment and facilities not readily available in peoples' homes. Still other programs make contact with their potential clients within the office of the sponsoring agency. Despite these differences in technique and location of program contact, all health, education, and welfare agencies must somehow solve the problem of bringing their services or technologies to their clients or client organizations. If these services or technologies cannot be brought to the clientele, then the clientele must be brought to the sponsoring agency. Here, program administrators and planners must concern themselves with the physical, material and social factors which prevent or facilitate program contact.

For the agencies that are more successful in recruiting applicants, the program contact stage may also involve screening out the applicant individuals, groups or organizations who are defined as ineligible for program benefits. Public welfare departments devote much of their staff time and effort to establishing and reestablishing the eligibility of welfare recipients. Teaching hospitals, in screening potential patients, give attention to whether patients' problems make for interesting teaching material. State mental hospitals should, ideally, concern themselves with screening out those potential patients who are not in need of institutionalization, or who would be more appropriately served by another facility, e.g., an institution for the retarded. On another level, organizations which formally certify professional schools give considerable attention to establishing the eligibility of teaching institutions, since only those schools that meet eligibility criteria receive certification.

The foregoing suggests that, despite their differences, all social programs are involved in the successful attainment of program contact. Administrators approach this with an eye to the program's ultimate goals and the availability of program resources. Some detailed examples of program contact follow.

Examples of Program Contact

Health: A TB control unit of a State Department of Health has as one of its purposes the reduction of tuberculosis in poor urban communities. Accomplishment of program contact requires the designated target population to receive chest x-rays. Past experience suggests, however, that a clinic program in a downtown public hospital is not successful in attracting the target population, since some of these people can not take the time or do not have the carfare to travel to the clinic, and others do not read about the program in the newspaper and consequently have no knowledge of it. Still others, perhaps suspecting that they have TB and fearful of the stigma or the treatment, are reluctant to be identified by public health officials. So, as an alternative program-contact strategy, program planners decide to institute a mobile x-ray unit to bring doctors, technicians and x-ray facilities directly to the client community. Other social agencies are informed of this new service and the dates when the mobile unit will be in the area. The time, effort and the social costs of the examinations are reduced and the visibility of the program is increased.

Education: An adult education program has as one of its purposes the improvement of the English language skills of recent, non-English-speaking immigrants. Program contact will necessitate decisions about how to inform the recent immigrants that the program is available, e.g., through advertisements in foreign-language newspapers, or contacts with appropriate nationality organizations. In addition, attention must be given to the physical location of the program and the times when classes are to be held. The merits of segregating nationality or language groups, versus mixing them in classes, will also have to be considered. Should the program be free to all participants, or should all participants pay a standard fee, or should the fee be determined on the basis of income? These decisions, and others as well, are likely to affect the success with which the program manages to contact its clientele.

Welfare: A settlement house decides to organize a welfare council in a given community. The goal is to coordinate the planning of the various social welfare agencies in the area. Program contact involves decisions about how to contact the potential member-agencies. How do the program's administrators communicate their objectives to decision-makers in the various organizations so that the program will present no threat and will offer some incentive for membership? Are meetings to be held in the sponsoring agency, or will they take place elsewhere in the community? Are meetings to be held at times when representatives of all significant agencies can attend? How the program planners answer these questions will significantly determine how well the program-contact stage is managed.

PROGRAM IMPLEMENTATION

Program implementation is the third stage of program development. In this final stage, the program fully engages its clientele and gives service and/or applies a change technology. The success of program implementation rests in part on the attainment of the necessary conditions of program initiation and contact. It also depends on the relevancy of the service offered or on the efficacy of the technology employed.

The purpose of the program-implementation stage is synonymous with the ultimate goals of the program. It is here that the *outcome* of agency activity can be measured. Questions about unanticipated positive and negative consequences of program interventions can also be answered during program implementation. In addition, this stage offers a locus in which the relative efficacy and efficiency of the program's various strategies can be evaluated.

In some programs, a necessary part of the implementation stage is the disengagement of clientele. Criteria for their discharge and a technology for handling it must be developed. A state mental hospital can be said to be truly successful only when it has successfully reintegrated its patients into the society. A job-training program for low-income people must be able to place trainees in meaningful positions where the skills they learned are, in fact, utilized. A correctional institution, to the extent that it focuses on rehabilitation, must concern itself with the reintegration of ex-convicts into the larger noncriminal community.

But disengagement can also be premature. It is possible, for example, that some organizations release their clientele before they are properly serviced or treated. Along these lines, some public welfare agencies have been accused of giving more attention to cutting clients off the welfare rolls than to servicing them. This issue suggests important questions for evaluation. More detailed examples follow.

Examples of Program Implementation

Health: A prenatal care clinic is set up for pregnant women in a low-income community. The goal of the program is to reduce the incidence of stillborn, premature, and defective infants in the area. The program director has acquired the resources successfully to initiate the program and to make contact with clientele. He is, however, concerned with the degree to which clients regularly keep their appointments, follow dietary instructions and other medical advice. Ultimately, of course, he is concerned with the extent to which there have been decreases in the birth rates of stillborn, premature, and defective infants in the area. Some secondary gains, which might result from the program, could involve improved health-care practices of the clients, such as the reduction of smoking or better dietary habits. In addition, the original clients might refer other women to the program, contributing to the program's success in contacting a larger potential clientele. Certain unanticipated negative consequences might result from an increased number of illegitimate children who might otherwise have died in childbirth: added pressures for families, schools, and other local institutions.

Education: A public-school system initiates a guidance and counseling program within its schools. Ample staff and material resources are available. Teachers have been cooperative and judicious in referring children with personal and social problems to the school guidance personnel. Ultimately, the question facing the program administrator is whether or not intervention has been successful in reducing school-related behavior problems. In addition, it would be helpful to find out whether behavior problems outside the context of the school were also reduced. In considering unanticipated negative consequences, it would be important to note whether teachers' classroom behavior has changed negatively as a result of the availability of the program. Have they become less tolerant of minor infractions of rules? Have they been less willing to work with children manifesting behavior difficulties? The program administrator might also investigate the differential effects of having the social workers function as consultants to the teachers, or as direct counselors to troubled youngsters.

Welfare: A food-stamp program is set up in a community, with the purpose of enabling local residents to have nutritionally adequate diets. The stamps, providing for foodstuffs which are compatible with the tastes and customs of the people in the area, are distributed regularly, and neighborhood food stores agree to accept the stamps. In this stage, the program director is interested in how people actually use the stamps, and whether the nutritional value of their diets does improve. In addition, it would be valuable to know whether or not participation in the program leads to greater interest in good nutrition and better planning in the selection of foods. On the negative side, one would want to know whether or not local stores raise their prices when stamps are distributed, and whether or not they allow customers to purchase nonprescribed products with their stamps, such as sweets, soft drinks, alcohol, etc.

DETERMINATION OF PROGRAM STAGES [1]

Although it is obvious that there are often no clear lines of demarcation between program stages, our purpose in delineating developmental stages is to make evaluation more relevant to the current state of a program. Differential evaluation then requires that the present developmental stage of the program be identified. But how can the program administrator make this determination? Listed below are some guidelines for identifying the developmental stage which dominates a social program.

1. How does the program allocate most of its staff time and resources? Are present efforts devoted to securing additional resources (initiation), recruiting clientele (contact), or giving service and/or applying a technology (implementation)?

---

[1] Many of the ideas in this section were derived from Amitai Etzioni, *Modern Organizations*, Prentice Hall, Inc., Englewood Cliffs, New Jersey, 1964.

2. When there are conflicts between the needs of the various program stages, how are these resolved? Which stage generally dominates?
3. What kinds of data and information does the program routinely collect? Does the intelligence system focus mainly on data concerning the availability of new program resources (initiation), description of clientele (contact), or impact on clientele of agency intervention (implementation)?
4. What kinds of staff activity receive the greatest economic and status rewards? What roles are viewed as most valuable to the program operation?
5. If there were a major cutback in funding, which functions would be sacrificed first, which last?

Each of the foregoing questions directs the administrator to a determination of the current "operative goals" of the program, and to the dominant stage of program development. These operative goals may coincide or depart from "stated" program goals, i.e., goals that are presented in formal program documents, mandates, contracts, and so forth. They do, however, tell the administrator where the program is at any point in time.

Chapter Three

OBJECTIVES OF DIFFERENTIAL EVALUATION

In Chapter Two, we described the three stages of program development: program initiation, program contact, and program implementation. The purpose of this chapter is to provide the program director with a framework for formulating evaluation objectives appropriate to the program's developmental stage. This framework is based on our notion of *differential evaluation,* which means simply that an evaluation of a social program should be geared primarily to the present stage of program development. In this context, different evaluation questions are suggested for different program stages; the range of evaluation techniques for answering these questions will be considered in the following chapter.

THE PROCESS OF DIFFERENTIAL
EVALUATION

Evaluation is a management technique for providing feedback of information to program administrators. Under ideal conditions, it is a continuous process which may involve more than one systematic collection of data and the use of more than one evaluation technique. Ultimately, social program evaluation seeks to compile information about achievements or failures in program implementation. However, achievement of overall program goals is often dependent on the success with which the problems of program initiation and contact have been managed. Some social programs never transcend the difficulties of dealing with these earlier developmental stages. In such programs, evaluation of program implementation alone would document the lack of ultimate program achievement, but would say little about the reasons why. Sometimes, external funding sources require routine evaluations before program implementation is even contemplated. Here again, an analysis of the effects of program interventions would be premature and relatively unproductive.

In attempting to make evaluation more relevant and responsive to program development, we are proposing the idea of differential evaluation. The process of differential evaluation involves delineating evaluation objectives which are appropriate to specific stages of program development, and matching evaluation techniques to these objectives. More precisely, a differential evaluation of a social program would necessarily include the following steps:

1. Specification of long-range and immediate operating goals and the means to accomplish these goals.
2. Determination of the current stage of program development, and collection of information about problems in attaining goals of former or subsequent program stages.
3. Formulation of evaluation objectives appropriate to the current stage of program development.
4. Selection of techniques of evaluation which will provide information relevant to evaluation objectives.
5. Review of information retrieved through evaluation, and translation into decisions about future program planning.
6. Repetition of the foregoing steps as the program expands, contracts, or otherwise changes.

EVALUATION OBJECTIVES

As we suggested above, differential evaluation involves the matching of evaluation objectives and techniques to program stages. Within each program stage,

however, three objectives or criteria of evaluation
should be considered: program effort, program effectiveness, and program efficiency. Essentially, then,
there are three basic objectives of program evaluation:

1. To provide descriptive information about the type
   and quantity of program activities (program
   effort).
2. To provide information about the achievement of
   the goals of the current stage of program development (program effectiveness).
3. To provide information about program effectiveness relative to program effort (program efficiency).

A program evaluation which does not include systematic information about effort, effectiveness, and efficiency is incomplete. For example, knowledge about
program efforts without corresponding knowledge
about the achievement of the goals of a particular stage
of development is relatively useless to the administrator
who must make decisions about continuing or altering
present strategies of intervention. He needs answers to
questions as to which activities should be increased or
curtailed; which activities bring about desired ends;
should there be a shift in program emphasis, etc.? Likewise, information about the achievement of program
objectives must be related to program effort. In this
way the administrator can make judgments about the
relative costs and efficiency of various intervention
strategies. Thus, the issues of effort, effectiveness, and

efficiency are different, but necessarily interrelated. Each of these criteria of evaluation will be discussed here.

Program Effort

Evaluation of program effort refers to an assessment of the amounts and kinds of program activities considered necessary for the accomplishment of program goals within a particular stage of development. It refers not only to staff time, activity, and commitment, but also to the allocation and use of material resources— funds, space, equipment, etc. For example, in a marital counseling program which is in the program contact stage, information such as the following might be obtained about program effort: what techniques for recruiting potential clientele have been employed; how much staff time, effort, funds, etc., have been expended; what ancillary resources have been used, e.g., outside consultation, media, public relations, etc.?

Program effort can be documented in any developmental stage. Essentially, this quantitative, descriptive information is an indication of the extent to which staff and program are active. Obviously, this says nothing about how well the tasks are being done, or, more importantly, whether or not the program's overall goals are attained. However, if there is little effort invested in a program, little can be accomplished; directors may be very interested in finding out whether or not staff are actively engaged in the program. Thus, program effort is necessary for the achievement of program goals, but evidence of program activity is not sufficient to determine whether or not these goals have been reached.

Information about program effort may be extremely useful to administrators in situations in which the relationship between intervention techniques and desired outcomes has been fairly firmly established. For example, a reading tutorial program has been set up to employ techniques of reading instruction that have been successfully initiated, and program contact has been made. An analysis of staff activity, however, reveals that staff is devoting a major proportion of its time and effort to recreational activities for individuals in the program. With this information, and after some thought to the reasons for the inappropriate character of staff activities (e.g., inadequate training in implementing the techniques of reading instruction), the administrator attempts to increase the proportion of staff time devoted to instructional activities. His decision is based on the assumption that these techniques of reading instruction will in fact lead to improved reading levels.

Of course, the program administrator may also be interested in evaluating the effectiveness of these techniques *within* his program. He may have reason to believe, for example, that the clientele served may be sufficiently different from that served in other programs (e.g., cultural or ethnic differences) so that the effectiveness of the means employed should not be taken as assumed. If he has information indicative of program effectiveness, he can be more certain of the correctness of his decisions about the allocation of agency resources.

Program Effectiveness

As with program effort, program effectiveness can be determined for any given stage of development. Effectiveness refers to the extent to which the goals of a particular stage have been achieved. For example, a community-based agency hopes to organize local resources to get a Model Cities Program operating in the area. In order to implement such a program, certain initiation activities must be successfully managed. A planning grant must be secured; a group of experts and local citizens must be brought together to document the need for such a project and plan a program; a representative board must be recruited and established; and so forth. Effectiveness in the initiation stage would refer to the success with which each of these foregoing requirements has been managed.

In addition to the above, an evaluation of effectiveness would consider both desirable and undesirable unanticipated consequences which may result from program activities. In the case of the initiation of a Model Cities Program, for example, an evaluator would be interested in the extent to which efforts for securing necessary resources to initiate such a program promoted either community cohesiveness or conflict. Are local residents becoming more active in community affairs unrelated to Model Cities? Are local community organizations and agencies fighting over available resources, or coordinating and integrating their programs and services?

Program effectiveness may also include information which bears on the achievement of program goals in relation to the need for the program. For example, each of two similar health programs in two different communities may have provided services to 100 families. One community (A) may have had 1,000 families in need of health services, while the other community (B) may have had 100 families which could benefit from health services. Thus, the services in community B are more comprehensive, in that the ratio between those served and those in need (100/100) is higher than it is for community A (100/1,000). Comprehensiveness is an index of effectiveness, which relates goal achievement to community needs.

Information regarding effectiveness is typically quantitative, but qualitative data which reflect on effectiveness may also be secured in program evaluations. For example, included in the objectives of some programs may be such items as the procurement of "adequate" physical facilities; compliance with regulations and local ordinances regarding discrimination, equal opportunity practices, personnel policies and housing codes; the procurement of "adequate" ratios of staff to people served, such as those for teachers and students, physicians and patients. Such information is often judged by the standards of professionals, who may base their judgments on previous experience, knowledge, and current professional norms. Those kinds of data are more often utilized in evaluating some objectives in the program initiation and contact stages of development. However, qualitative information is also used in evaluating the effectiveness of program implementation.

Two alternative program approaches may lead to the same degree of effectiveness, but the expenditure of resources in one program may be greater than in the other. An important item of information for the administrator, then, is the relative cost for accomplishing program objectives. Other things being equal, the administrator would choose that program which is the least costly in terms of time, money, manpower, and other resources. Thus, program efficiency is another important object of evaluation.

Program Efficiency

Program efficiency focuses on the relationship between efforts and effectiveness. It is the ratio of effectiveness to effort, and it is concerned with the relative costs for achieving program objectives. Costs include expenditures of manpower, time, money, physical facilities and so forth.

Questions regarding efficiency are familiar to administrators who are involved in making programmatic decisions within the constraints of relatively fixed budgets. Evaluation of efficiency often involves comparison of two or more different techniques (or strategies, or programs) with respect to their relative costs and program outcomes. However, questions may also be raised about duplications of effort, irrespective of whether or not one has knowledge of the effectiveness of those efforts. To illustrate the point, a program may employ 10 persons to determine whether applicants are eligible for its services. If all 10 persons interview the *same* applicants, there is an unnecessary duplication of efforts. The less duplication of effort, the more efficient the program. The notion of duplication of efforts can be expanded to include office procedures, the use of meetings and committees, and so forth.

As indicated previously, questions of efficiency need not be focused directly on financial costs. For example, the use of time is important information for the administrator. How much time is spent in the teaching of groups as opposed to tutorials? Can an interview devoted to determining eligibility of program applicants be concluded in one hour as opposed to three hours?

The essence of an evaluation of efficiency is highlighted in this question: can the same program results be achieved by *either* reducing the amount of program effort *or* by choosing other, less costly alternatives (different kinds of efforts)?

EVALUATION QUESTIONS AND PROGRAM DEVELOPMENT

The objective of differential evaluation is to produce sets of data on the efforts, effectiveness, and efficiency of achieving program goals. Evaluation questions which are geared to different stages of development represent specifications of this objective. In order to illustrate more systematically the linkage between the stages of development and the evaluation questions, the following section offers some evaluation questions that can be asked of social programs in the different development stages. The questions are intended to serve as illustrative guidelines. Prior to the delineation of more general evaluation questions, we also offer brief examples of evaluation questions applied to specific social programs.

Program Initiation

As was discussed in Chapter Two, the goals in the program-initiation stage are concentrated on securing the necessary resources and conditions for client contact and program implementation. An example of a social program in the initiation stage might be a job-training program which is proposed for public-welfare recipients in a particular community, with the ultimate goal of helping recipients to be financially independent.

Immediate goals in the initiation stage are focused on the selection and recruitment of competent staff, the determination of necessary criteria for eligibility, etc. To formulate evaluation objectives it is necessary to specify questions which are related to the effort, effectiveness, and efficiency with which the tasks of the initiation stage are managed. Questions such as the following might be raised to evaluate program efforts: what attempts were made to secure staff persons to operate the program; how much time, energy, and other resources were devoted to the specification of eligibility criteria, such as the educational level necessary to benefit from the program; and so forth?

Questions regarding program effectiveness are related to the extent to which program efforts result in the achievement of program goals. Thus, the following questions of effectiveness can be raised: were sufficient numbers of staff persons hired in accordance with their planned qualifications; are criteria developed for the unbiased selection of program participants; are adequate accounting, bookkeeping and social data-recording procedures established?

Program efficiency of the job-training program might be evaluated with respect to questions such as these: if different methods for the recruitment of staff are used, which method is most efficient in terms of length of time for recruitment and the costs of program efforts; to what extent is the content of training relevant to the job market (e.g., training for secretarial work when no jobs in the community are available for secretaries)?

Illustrative Evaluation Questions: Program Initiation

EFFORT

1. How much time and energy are devoted to the recruitment of staff for the program?
2. What is the extent and the type of activity which is devoted to the location of resources and the procurement of program cooperation?
3. What is the extent of involvement in the development of personnel policies and practices, and adequate accounting, bookkeeping, and data-collection procedures?
4. What are the number and nature of activities devoted to the development of an operational plan, the review of existing programs of a similar nature, a review of the literature for alternative approaches, and interviews with persons who have experience in similar programs?
5. To what extent are efforts made to locate the anticipated target population?
6. What efforts are focused on the learning of statutes, ordinances, and regulations which are relevant to the program?

EFFECTIVENESS

1. Are there any staff vacancies; how many of the filled positions are a result of recruiting efforts?

2. To what extent does the program meet a community need? To what extent can potential participants be identified; would those persons be willing to participate in the program?
3. To what extent is a program plan specified, including its objectives and alternative ways to accomplish those objectives?
4. To what extent are budgeting, accounting and data collection procedures established in accordance with acceptable practices?
5. To what extent are personnel policies and practices explicated and consistent with relevant laws and guidelines?
6. To what extent are staff functions and responsibilities delineated?

EFFICIENCY

1. What are the relative costs of different techniques for the recruitment of staff?
2. In comparison with existing programs of a similar nature, what are the relative costs for the initiation stage of the program?
3. To what extent are staff salaries commensurate with the responsibilities of staff positions, in relation to similar jobs in the community?
4. What are the relations between program efforts and program effectiveness; what proportions of staff time and resources are spent in relation to achieved goals?

5. To what extent are there duplicated staff functions which could result in possible ambiguity and conflict?

6. To what extent do staff persons perceive program objectives as similar or dissimilar; to what extent do staff persons have competing objectives which are at cross purposes with one another?

Program Contact

The goals of the contact stage are concerned with the bringing together of program content and clientele. Immediate objectives are focused on the identification of favorable and unfavorable conditions for program contacts. Accordingly, evaluation questions are geared to the efforts, effectiveness, and efficiency with which program contact is managed. For example, a social program in the contact stage might be one in which a public health program is initiated for the purpose of locating and treating venereal disease in the teenage population. Evaluation questions related to effort are as follows: how much manpower time is expended to reach the target population; what techniques and media are used to make initial contact; and so forth?

Effectiveness might be assessed by providing answers to questions such as these: what proportion of the target population knows about the program; how willing are they to come in for initial examinations, etc.?

Questions of efficiency are those which involve the relation of staff efforts to the achievement of the goal of client contact. Are there less costly, but equally or more effective, uses of media and modes of dissemination of information, uses of staff, etc. for contacting clientele?

Illustrative Evaluation Questions: Program Contact

EFFORT

1. What amounts of time, energy and program resources are devoted to making program contacts with intended beneficiaries: number of interviews, etc.?
2. If a referral system is used, what is the amount of time and effort involved in referrals?
3. What efforts are devoted to the compilation of records pertaining to program activity?
4. What amounts of time and energy are devoted to finding resources which could increase the number of program contacts?
5. To what extent are alternative program strategies sought and utilized, if program efforts do not appear sufficient to reach all of the intended target population?

EFFECTIVENESS

1. To what extent is the intended target population represented in those who are designated as program beneficiaries?

2. What are the opinions of the intended target population regarding the extent to which the content of the program is reaching them, and the reasons why program contacts are or are not made?

3. What is the relative effectiveness of various techniques used to make contacts with the program's clientele?

4. What is the number of appropriate services used, out of the possible number of available referral sources; what are the reasons for the use (or lack of use) of referral services?

5. What happens to prospective clientele who are referred to other programs; how many persons follow through on their referrals; how many persons actually receive services from the programs to which they are referred?

EFFICIENCY

1. What are the relative proportions of staff time devoted to program objectives, and to what extent is the use of staff time related to the achievement of those objectives?

2. What are the relative costs of using different means for contacting clientele?

3. Are staff functions and roles structured to maximize program consistency for the achievement of program goals?

4. Are certain client characteristics more related to

program contact than others; e.g., do whites receive more or less program contact than blacks?

5. Are certain staff characteristics more related to program contacts than others; e.g., do whites receive more or less program contact from white or black staff members?

Program Implementation

Program implementation involves the achievement of, or failure to achieve, overall program goals. For an education program which attempts to increase the education level of adults from below third-grade to an eighth-grade level, evaluation questions of effort might include the following: how many hours of instruction were provided for what specific skills, such as reading and arithmetic; what devices were considered, and actually used, for assessing the educational level of program beneficiaries; and so forth?

Questions of effectiveness might include the following: how many program beneficiaries actually increased their educational levels in reading, arithmetic, etc.; what proportion of the intended target population increased their educational levels; and how many persons dropped out of the program and for what reasons?

Efficiency might be appraised by seeking information through questions such as these: is group teaching less costly and equally as effective as tutorials; could the same degree of effectiveness be obtained by less costly means through the use of non-professional teachers, teaching machines, etc.?

Illustrative Evaluation Questions:

Program Implementation

EFFORT

1. How much time and energy are devoted to a review of staff objectives and activities?
2. What staff efforts are involved in the respecification of goals, and in the location of additional resources judged necessary to achieve program results?
3. How much effort is devoted to the specification of criteria for program termination and necessary follow-up activities?
4. How much time and energy are devoted to the procurement of follow-up information from program beneficiaries?

EFFECTIVENESS

1. What results have been achieved which could be attributed to the program; are there discernible changes in the knowledge, attitudes or skills of the program beneficiaries; are there changes in behavior on the part of individuals, groups or organizations?

2. What results could have been obtained without the content of the program (would changes have taken place anyway)?
3. Are there any unplanned outcomes, either desirable or undesirable, that could be attributed to the program?
4. What is the relative effectiveness of the program compared with other programs that have similar objectives?
5. How effective is the program in relation to the need of the intended target population for the content of the program (services, etc.)?

EFFICIENCY

1. What are the relative costs of different techniques used to achieve similar results?
2. What is the relation of costs of program effort to the benefits of results achieved?
3. What are the relative costs of the program in comparison with other programs with similar objectives?
4. Could the same results be achieved with a reduction in program efforts?

Chapter Four

TECHNIQUES OF EVALUATION

After the evaluation objectives have been specified, the next concern in differential evaluation is the selection of appropriate techniques which can be used to provide relatively unbiased information pertinent to the questions of evaluation. Although the typical administrator is not an expert in evaluation techniques, he is often in a position where he must seek consultation regarding the kind of evaluation strategy that is most appropriate for his program. The task of the administrator is to locate an evaluation expert who is able to select and/or use those techniques, or combinations of techniques, which would yield the desired information at reasonable cost. In order to locate and use evaluation experts appropriately, however, the administrator should have some acquaintance with the aims of various evaluation techniques.

Accordingly, our goal in this chapter is to acquaint the administrator with the aims of various evaluation techniques. Each of the techniques can be used at different stages of evaluation, for providing information regarding efforts, effectiveness, and efficiency of program goals. These techniques are grouped into three categories: monitoring techniques, social-research techniques, and cost-analytic techniques. *Monitoring techniques* include those procedures which are used for the direct review of program operations: accountability audit, administrative audit, and time-and-motion studies. *Social-research techniques* refer to those procedures, exclusive of cost considerations, that are used for developing, modifying, and expanding knowledge about the program which can be communicated and verified by independent investigators: experiment, survey, and case study. *Cost-analytic techniques* are those procedures which are used to appraise the relative value of a program in relation to program costs: cost accounting, cost-benefit analyses, cost-outcome analyses, and operations research, which blends experimental and cost-analytic methods.

These categories of techniques are overlapping, but they are useful because particular kinds of evaluation experts are often identified with these groupings. Thus, management consultants, accountants, efficiency experts, organizational sociologists, and statisticians may be associated with monitoring techniques; psychologists, sociologists, bio-statisticians, and epidemiologists with social-research techniques; and accountants, economists, mathematicians, and systems analysts with cost-analytic techniques.

The purpose of this chapter is to present ten selected evaluation techniques, and to include in our brief discussions of each technique the following: a description of the technique including its purpose, what experts in the techniques are likely to do, the kinds of knowledge which can be produced by the technique, and an indication of the relative costs in terms of time, money, and manpower; a discussion of some suggested *uses* of the technique in relation to the objects of evaluation and different stages of program development; and a list of *selected references* from which the reader can derive more detailed discussions of the technique.

MONITORING TECHNIQUES

Accountability Audit

DESCRIPTION

Accountability-audit techniques are used to review the consistency, dependability, and accuracy of records pertaining to program expenditures, allocations of resources, and processing of program beneficiaries, for the purpose of establishing program accountability. These are essentially methods for reviewing two kinds of accounting records: general and social.

General accounting refers to the program's system for keeping track of program costs, including payroll, purchasing, and so forth. An audit (review) of general accounting procedures is conducted typically by an auditor, or an experienced accountant, versed in the operations of programs similar to the one which he is reviewing. The auditor attempts to verify the accuracy of the recorded financial status of the program. In addition, he seeks to determine whether the general accounting system used by the program is sufficiently monitored by relevant staff—that the assets of the program are safeguarded, the accuracy and reliability of accounting data are maintained, and the prescribed managerial and operating procedures are followed. The auditor locates written policies regarding the accounting procedures, and he may interview those staff persons who perform accounting functions to obtain an overview of the flow of information concerning the program's cost procedures, and determine whether or not there are mechanisms for internal verification of the accuracy of those procedures. The auditor then may look at the accounting books that are maintained, and make a judgment as to whether those books (such as a cash and in-kind receipts journal) are in accordance with acceptable general accounting procedures. Finally, he reviews the accounts for accuracy and consistency.

The knowledge obtained by an audit of general accounting consists of verification of the program's system, and recommendations for improving the dependability of the program's accounting procedures. The costs involved are primarily the salaries of one or more auditors for a brief period of time, perhaps one or two weeks. However, the costs obviously depend on the scope and complexity of the program's general accounting procedures, and the extent to which those procedures are developed. Assistance initially in setting up accounting procedures, for example, may be less costly than later finding an error in the system and recommending a more dependable, but different, system of accounting.

Social accounting refers to the methods used by the program for recording and keeping track of program beneficiaries. It is this accounting system which is the source of program statistics on such things as how many persons were contacted by program staff, where contacts were made, and so forth. The auditing might be done by a systems analyst, statistician, epidemiologist, or social researcher who is expert in the formulation and use of program records for processing client information. The auditing function involves an appraisal of the existence, reliability, and accuracy of the program's procedures for reporting on those persons who have been processed through the program—from recruiting and program-contact efforts to final follow-up. The auditor looks at the available records in use, such as monthly or daily activity reports; files kept for such records; and any reported statistics regarding program progress. Then he checks the records which form the basis for the reported statistics to verify their accuracy. In addition, he may review policies, procedures, and definitions of statistical categories. The auditor attempts to determine whether or not definitions are ambiguous, and whether or not there appears to be an accurate count of people processed through the program. Where numbers are used, but based on varying estimates without documentation, he makes a judgment regarding the validity of such numbers (e.g., when a recreation program reports that it has processed 10,000 people at a public park during a given month—is that figure based on information which indicates 10,000 different people, or is it the number of days in a month multiplied by how many people a recreation worker believed were at the park on a given day?).

The knowledge obtained from an audit of social accounting includes recommendations for an adequate data-processing system. These record-keeping systems contain basic kinds of information which are essential for program planning, development, and review. The more thorough the system, from intake through follow-up, the more costly it will be. The costs of a social-accounting expert for a review are not exorbitant, but a comprehensive data-recording system is not cheap. Much information can be manufactured and processed through a computerized data-collection system, but, if information is collected without being used, the cost is excessive and unnecessary. Therefore, the role of the auditor is to recommend which kinds of information pertinent to program goals and evaluation objectives should be collected.

USES

Accountability-audit techniques can be used to provide information which bears on efforts, effectiveness, and efficiency of program goals during the three stages of program development. For example, a review of a social program in the initiation stage may indicate whether or not program efforts have been devoted to the establishment of general and social accounting procedures, how effective the program has been in employing an adequate accounting system, and how efficient the system is in terms of duplication of efforts and so forth.

A program in the contact stage cannot have adequate knowledge of its efforts and effectiveness unless the documentation exists in its social accounting records. Thus, accountability-audit techniques can determine whether or not the program has the necessary procedures for the efficient tabulation of those clients who are processed by the program.

For programs in the implementation stage, administrators often have difficulty in securing follow-up information pertinent to those who have graduated from their program. Accountability-audit techniques can be used for recommending ways to process follow-up information. Moreover, they can be used to review the program's efforts to procure such information for data processing.

REFERENCES[1]

1. Bauer, Raymond A., Ed., *Social Indicators,* The M.I.T. Press, Cambridge, Massachusetts, 1966.

   A selection of five articles which deal with the use and planning of social statistical data. Especially recommended for the reader are the sections on "Social Indicators and Goals" by Albert D. Biderman, pp. 68–153, and "The State of the Nation: Social Systems Accounting" by Bertram M. Gross, pp. 154–271.

2. Hill, John G., "Cost Analysis of Social Work Service," in *Social Work Research,* Ed., Norman A. Polansky, The University of Chicago Press, 1960, pp. 223–246.

   Distinctions between general accounting and cost accounting are discussed, and examples of accounting principles for health and welfare agencies are presented.

3. Office of Economic Opportunity Community Action Program, *Guide for Grantee Accounting,* Office of Program

---

[1] The references included in this and subsequent sections are not intended to be exhaustive. They are principal sources for the authors, and they are merely intended to be suggestive to the reader who wants to delve more deeply into each technique.

Review, Community Action Program, Washington, D.C., 36 pp., 1966.

This pamphlet proposes guidelines for adequate general accounting systems for a variety of social programs funded by the Office of Economic Opportunity. It is prepared especially as an aid for program directors of small scale, newly organized programs.

4. Sherwood, Clarence C., "Guidelines for a Data Collection System for Community Programs for Unemployed Youth," paper prepared for New York University Graduate School of Social Work, Center for the Study of Unemployed Youth, February, 1966, 16 pp.

Specific recommendations are made for a data collection system relevant to the social accountability of social programs.

5. Terry, George R., *Principles of Management*, Fifth Edition, Richard D. Irwin, Inc., Homewood, Illinois, 1968.

This is a comprehensive text on principles of management. In particular, Chapter 22 on "Managerial Controlling" and Chapter 23 on "Overall Managerial Controls and Audits" are essential sources for background information on principles of general accounting as used in business

organizations. The principles discussed
are applicable to the financial and general accounting operations of social programs.

Administrative Audit

DESCRIPTION

Administrative-audit techniques are those methods
which attempt to describe what is done by staff in
relation to standards established by sources external
and/or internal to the program. Standards are designated norms of desirable activity, and they may
be derived from the professions or other groups; or
relative standards may be derived from a systematic
comparison with other similar programs or organizations. More specifically, administrative-audit techniques,
herein, refer to those methods used to evaluate the suitability of program policies, and practices directed toward compliance with those policies; to evaluate the
adherence of staff practices to designated divisions of
responsibility and function; and to evaluate the organizational patterns of work in terms of preferred and
efficient procedures within the program and/or between the program and other programs of a similar
nature.

An administrative auditor might be a management
consultant, an expert on administrative procedures, an
expert on intraorganizational procedures and systems

engineering, or a sociologist who is expert in comparing complex organizations. A comprehensive and detailed administrative audit might require a team of those experts, or one or more persons who have a combination of skills such as the analysis of management procedures within and between organizations.

An administrative audit might contain any of the following ingredients. The auditor looks for written policies regarding personnel practices, functions, and responsibilities. He may determine whether or not organizational charts are used, and to what extent existing staff practices may correspond with those charts. In addition, he looks for internal consistencies and inconsistencies as reflected in the chart, and observes whether or not such ambiguities are reflected in the interviews he conducts with staff and in the observations he makes. Moreover, he attempts to determine the degree of consistency among those staff members he interviews regarding their perceptions of staff functions and responsibilities. Available documents (written policies, codes, minutes of staff meetings, board meeting minutes, etc.) are reviewed with respect to internal consistency and their correspondence with available policies, ordinances, etc., outside of the program.

The knowledge obtained from an administrative audit is usually in the form of facts pertaining to administrative and staff work patterns, and the extent to which the program could improve its goals in relation to its management activities. The management audit can be more limited in perspective, and concentrate on developing knowledge which pertains to such things as civil rights compliance, adherence to nondiscriminatory personnel practices, and recommendations for more efficient staff efforts. With a limited audit, the costs are minimal; namely, those of manpower necessary for the audit over a brief period of time. On the other hand, considerable costs are entailed in comprehensive audits which include the use of a variety of specific techniques (such as PERT, as described in the reference below, to assist in planning the accomplishment of specific tasks in given amounts of time) for appraising the program administration over extended periods of time, and for comparing it with other similar programs.

USES

The information secured by administrative-audit techniques is particularly useful for the planning involved in social programs. Although an administrative audit may be helpful in all stages of program development, it is more useful in the program-initiation and contact stages. As previously indicated, the information gathered by the auditor may be used to form judgments, based on available documentation, regarding discriminatory practice toward employees, lack of compliance with specified regulations, personnel conflicts in the operation of the program, lack of compliance with accepted professional practices, and so forth. Recommendations can then be made concerning the efforts that the program should make in order to be more effective and efficient in its administrative practices. For example, a management audit of the initiation stage of an anti-poverty program may reveal the extent to which the program made efforts to secure adequate representation on its policy and planning board (door-to-door house canvassing, advertisements in the media for local elections, etc.); the extent to which recruiting efforts were effective in being nondiscriminatory; and the program's efficiency (unnecessary duplication) in its hiring procedures.

A more comprehensive administrative audit may include recommendations for estimating the number of personnel necessary for providing effective services, as determined by professional judgments of adequate service (e.g., see reference below by Schonfeld *et al.*), or a comparative analysis of the program's administrative efforts, effectiveness, and efficiency with other programs (e.g., see references below by Perrow, Fanshel, and Terry).

REFERENCES

1. Etzioni, Amitai, *Modern Organizations*, Prentice Hall, Inc., Englewood Cliffs, New Jersey, 1964.

An excellent and succinct text which presents and reviews concepts for the analysis of complex organizations. In particular, Chapter Two which includes a discussion of the nature of organizational goals and their evaluation is important background information regarding the nature of different organizations.

2. Fanshel, David, Ed., *Research in Social Welfare Administration: Its Contributions and Problems,* National Association of Social Workers, New York, New York, 1962.

This text includes discussions of major issues regarding research of administration in social work and several suggested techniques for the analysis of different administrative structures. Recommended for the reader are these articles: "The Study of Organizational Effectiveness" by Herman D. Stein, pp. 22–32, and "Research in Administrative Medicine: Comparative Analysis of Systems of Health Service Organizations" by Milton I. Roemer, pp. 72–83.

3. Perrow, Charles, "A Framework for the Comparative Analysis of Organizations," *American Sociological Review,* Vol. 32, No. 2, April, 1967, pp. 194–208.

A suggested framework for comparing different social organizations is proposed and discussed.

4. Pfeiffer, John, *New Look at Education: Systems Analysis in Our Schools and*

Colleges, Odyssey Press, Poughkeepsie, New York, 1968.

An interesting and informative discussion of techniques used for analyzing educational institutions. In particular, clear discussions of PERT and other critical path methods for determining efficient and effective time schedules for the completion of projects are presented in Chapter Three, pp. 33–53.

5. Schonfeld, H. K., Falk, I. S., Lavietes, P. H., Landwirth, I., and Krassnor, L. S., "The Development of Standards for the Audit and Planning of Medical Care," *American Journal of Public Health,* Vol. 88, No. 11, November, 1968, pp. 2097–2110.

The authors describe a technique for deriving and applying standards of good pediatric care for estimating the number of personnel needed to provide adequate care.

6. Terry, George R., *Principles of Management,* Fifth Edition, 1968, Richard D. Irwin, Inc., Homewood, Illinois.

Recommended are Chapter Seven on "Management Planning," Chapter 20 on "Evaluating and Developing Management Members" and Chapter 22 on "Managerial Control." These chapters

contain a variety of techniques used for
the management audit of business organizations.

Time-and-Motion Studies

DESCRIPTION

Time-and-motion studies refer to those methods
which attempt to describe the use of time by program
staff and administrators in relation to the activities in
which they are involved. Information in these studies
may be obtained from samples of program activity
during selected periods of time; it might also contain
reports by staff members on written forms, observations
of and interviews with the staff, and the relationship
of descriptions of actual staff activity to planned staff
functions. The purposes of these methods are to specify
the total amounts of time devoted by staff to program
activities, to locate the uses of staff time which were
not anticipated, and to recommend reallocations of
staff time to those activities which might be more directly related to the potential achievement of program
goals.

These studies are typically conducted by auditors,
particularly administrative auditors (or management
analysts) and cost accountants, who combine time-and-
motion studies with studies of cost (see reference below
by Elkin). Experts in the use of these methods attempt
to obtain accurate information which is centered on

time as the unit of measurement. Although time can be measured accurately by the use of a stop watch in combination with observations of staff activity, many of these studies do not require such precise documentation to obtain an overall perspective of what amounts of time are devoted to what activities. Typically, self-reports by staff, over selected representative periods of time, are the primary data which are obtained. Thus, the procedures used are relatively inexpensive when self-reports are used. In addition, for large, complex programs, the costs can be reduced by using sampling methods (see references included in survey techniques in this chapter). For example, to describe the use of time during a given month, two weeks may be randomly selected. Following that selection, two half-day periods from each week may be chosen. Then, on those designated half days, staff may complete questionnaires on the way in which their time is spent on an hourly basis. Of course, the sampling and the unit of time selected vary depending upon the complexity and diversity of the program. Nevertheless, reasonably reliable information can be obtained within a short period of time at minimal costs.

USES

Time-and-motion studies are used primarily to describe the amounts of time devoted to program efforts. They are also useful as an indication of program efficiency with respect to time. The auditor may locate duplications of effort or excessive amounts of time spent on activities which may not be related to program goals.

These studies can be used for all stages of program development. In fact, as indicated earlier, the way in which staff time is allocated may give an indication of the stage of development toward which a program is moving. Moreover, a time-and-motion study may reveal whether or not a program is devoting necessary manpower to specified goals for its current stage of development. For example, a great deal of staff activity devoted to the recruitment of new staff when the program has already achieved that particular objective could be viewed as inefficient if the program is in the contact stage of development.

REFERENCES

1. Elkin, Robert, "Analyzing Time, Costs, and Operations in a Voluntary Children's Institution and Agency," Project on Cost Analysis in Children's Institutions, North Building, U.S. Department of Health, Education, and Welfare, Washington, D.C., September, 1965, pp. 27–39.

This is a study of a children's institution which uses a cost-analysis procedure recommended by the Child Welfare League of America. Included in the study is a section devoted to the use of time by personnel and the percentage of that time which is directed to the care and treatment of individual children.

2. Hill, John G., "Cost Analysis of Social Work Service," in *Social Work Research*, Ed., Norman A. Polansky, The University of Chicago Press, 1960, pp. 238–242.

   In the designated pages above the author discusses the notion of time sampling as used in a study of social services in Philadelphia.

3. Terry, George R., *Principles of Management*, Fifth Edition, Richard D. Irwin, Inc., Homewood, Illinois, 1968.

   Chapter 25, "Controlling Time Use and Cost," pp. 604–612, discusses the use of time and its control by management.

SOCIAL RESEARCH TECHNIQUES

Experiments

DESCRIPTION

The purpose of experiments is to provide evidence as to whether or not program efforts are related causally to the accomplishment of program goals. Logical procedures are employed for setting up experimental arrangements and the collection of data such that inferences can be made about the effects of the program. In a frequently used model of experimentation, the *classical experimental design,* objectives of the program and the means to accomplish those objectives are specified and standardized. Criterion variables which are considered relevant to the effects of a program are defined precisely so they can be measured. The target population is determined, and a representative sample of that population is secured through probability sampling techniques. The members of the sample are assigned randomly to experimental (one or more groups that receive program efforts) and control groups (one or more groups that are similar to the experimental group with respect to all relevant characteristics except that they do not receive efforts of the program or efforts from other programs that are similar). Finally, the groups are measured before and after program intervention and compared, with respect to change, on the criterion variables.

The data used in experiments may be obtained from questionnaires, observations of behavior, self-reports, interviews, tests, ratings, and so forth. The information gathered is for the purpose of showing change which can be attributed primarily to the program: for example, the procurement of jobs by welfare recipients, completing school, reduction of physical and mental symptoms of disturbance, changes in attitudes, and so forth.

Experimentalists are those persons who are expert in the formulation and application of experimental methods. Those experts usually have secured their training in experimental methods in sociology or psychology and/or in applied statistical and bio-statistical methods. The problems which must be solved by the experimenter, in conjunction with program personnel, include specifying program intervention which is presumably related to program effects, delineating who or what is to receive program intervention and for what period of time, the inclusion of adequate control groups, and the specification of measurable variables which provide valid and reliable information pertaining to those effects which could be attributed to the program being evaluated.

Experimentalists, in many instances, cannot use the classical experimental design because ideal experimental arrangements are not possible or practical. Therefore, those experts may devise quasi-experiments or approximations to experiments. For example, instead of a control group as used in the classical experimental design, comparative groups such as the following may be used:

1. a group that is similar to the experimental group on many relevant variables is selected after the experimental group has received program intervention.
2. a group which is similar to the experimental group but receives less frequent program efforts rather than no program intervention.

In approximations to experiments there is less certainty of the knowledge obtained than in true experiments, but useful evidence pertaining to cause-effect assertions can be gathered. In the references below by Hyman and Campbell and Stanley, a variety of experiments and approximations to experiments are discussed with respect to the certainty of knowledge that can be produced.

Experiments used to evaluate comprehensive social programs involve extensive periods of time for their execution and analysis. More rigor is included than in other research procedures, and this means that program goals and operations must be relatively standardized. In addition, after the program intervention is terminated, follow-up information on program beneficiaries should be obtained to determine whether observed changes are temporary or long lasting. Although comprehensive program experiments are costly, the knowledge produced from experiments may not be obtainable by any other means.

USES

Experiments are used primarily for evaluating the effects of programs which are in the implementation stage. For example, a program on reading disability might be evaluated with respect to the reduction of reading disabilities in a group which receives program intervention, as compared to a group which has reading disabilities but does not receive any program efforts. If reading disabilities are reduced more frequently in the experimental group and if it can be demonstrated that the possible effects of other variables are controlled, then it might be inferred that the program is effective with respect to the criterion of the reduction of reading disabilities.

Experiments also can be employed for other stages of development. For example, in the program-contact stage, two or more different methods for involving program recipients may be compared with a control group to determine which methods are effective, and which method is the most efficient in terms of greater effectiveness for its efforts. Or the same method may be employed, but two or more comparison groups are used to determine the extent to which intensity of contacts (e.g., number of interviews with potential program participants) yields similar or greater results. Thus, experiments can be used to determine the relative efficiency of program efforts for any of the three stages of development. They deal primarily with effects, but they can be used to indicate the relative efficiency of different amounts and kinds of program effort. They are not used for determining whether or not program efforts have been achieved.

REFERENCES

1. Campbell, Donald T. and Stanley, Julian C., "Experimental and Quasi-experimental Designs for Research on Teaching," in *Handbook of Research on Teaching*, N. A. Gage, Ed., Rand McNally and Co., Chicago, 1963, pp. 171–246.

This is a classic treatise on principles of control in experimentation. A variety of experimental designs with their advantages and disadvantages is presented. Examples are from education, but the principles of experimentation also apply to social programs in health and welfare.

2. Fairweather, George W., *Methods for Experimental Social Innovation*, John Wiley & Sons, Inc., New York, 1967.

This text discusses in detail the necessary steps for the planning of experiments to compare alternative approaches as solutions to social problems.

3. Hyman, Herbert H., Wright, Charles R., and Hopkins, Terence K., *Applications of Methods of Evaluation*, University of California Press, Berkeley and Los Angeles, 1962.

Four evaluative research studies of The Encampment for Citizenship, a social program, are presented. In Part I on "Principles of Evaluation," pp. 3–85, the authors discuss experimental design and approximations to experimental design which they employed in their studies. Their discussion of evaluation is excellent.

4. Suchman, Edward A., *Evaluative Re-*

search: Principles and Practice in Public Service and Social Action Programs, Russell Sage Foundation, New York, New York, 1967.

This is a text on evaluative research which includes a variety of examples from the field of public health. Experimental methods are emphasized and clarified in Chapter Five, "The Conduct of Evaluative Research," Chapter Six, "The Evaluative Research Design," and Chapter Seven, "The Measurement of Effects."

Surveys

DESCRIPTION

Survey methods are those methods which aim to yield facts which are descriptive of a social program. Included among these facts are the accurate description of the target population (i.e., that population which a program intends to benefit) with respect to attitudes, opinions, and reported changes in behavior. In addition to the descriptive function of the accumulation of accurate facts and statements of opinion which are representative of the target population, surveys may also have an explanatory function, which may be accomplished by such devices as the analysis of many variables simultaneously, as in multivariate analysis (see reference by Hyman below), or by surveys of comparative groups, as in quasi-experiments or approximations to experiments. For example, those who have heart disease are compared with those who do not, with respect to cigarette smoking and other kinds of habits and characteristics, in an effort to locate possible causal connections between other factors and heart disease.

A survey typically involves the designation of a target population; the selection of a representative sample from that population, using techniques of probability sampling (see reference below by Hess *et al.*); the collection of data, primarily from constructed questionnaires or interview schedules; the use of procedures to verify the accuracy of the accumulated information and to minimize response and interviewer biases; and the processing and analysis of data. Analyses are conducted in relation to the objectives of the survey, the completion of information, and available techniques of data processing.

Experts in survey techniques are usually social scientists, such as sociologists or social psychologists with special training in survey methods, public opinion and market research specialists, or epidemiologists and biostatisticians who have had their training in public health and mathematics or statistics. In addition, they may be attached to reputable survey-research centers within universities such as Michigan, Columbia, and

Chicago, or in private business such as the Gallup organization.

The survey is a flexible technique, and it can be adapted to fit varying cost budgets. It can provide simple descriptive facts more quickly than experiments, and it is less costly than experiments when it is used to provide evidence for hypotheses related to social programs. However, although representative samples are more often obtained in surveys than in experiments, experiments have greater degrees of control for ruling out the influence of variables other than program efforts which could be responsible for observed changes in program beneficiaries. The most efficient aspect of surveys is the use of sampling procedures. Results from a sample can be used to generalize to the total target population, and the expert use of this procedure can result in reduced costs. Nevertheless, a good survey involves necessary expenses: the sample selection; the construction and pretesting of appropriate interview schedules; the training and hiring of interviewers; data processing; and so forth. Depending upon the scope and desired accuracy of the survey, some costs can be reduced—for example, by using program staff as interviewers.

USES

Survey techniques can be used in all stages of program development. During the initiation of a program, survey techniques can be used to determine the need for the program on the part of people in designated communities, the incidence and prevalence of disease, low literacy rates, malnutrition, inadequate housing, and so forth.

In the program-contact stage, survey methods can be used to describe the extent to which program personnel are making efforts to involve program beneficiaries. Moreover, the effectiveness of these efforts can be determined. For example, the proportion of the target population that is contacted by the program can be estimated and related to the program goals. Moreover, survey techniques can be combined with cost-analytic techniques and time-and-motion studies to form estimates of the program's efficiency.

Survey methods can be used as approximations to experiments to provide evidence which bears on the total effectiveness of the social program. For example, data such as the percentage of the target population which was contacted, processed through a job-training program, and placed in jobs might be critical information for evaluating the effectiveness of the job-training program.

REFERENCES

1. Glock, Charles Y., Ed., *Survey Research in the Social Sciences*, Russell Sage Foundation, New York, 1967.

A collection of articles is presented on the uses of survey research in a variety of disciplines. In particular, these articles are recommended: "Education and Survey Research" by Martin Trow, pp. 315–376; "The Survey Method in Social Work: Past, Present, and Potential," by Fred Massarika, pp. 377–422, and "The Survey Method Applied to Public Health and Medicine" by Edward A. Suchman, pp. 423–519.

2. Hayes, Samuel P., Jr., *Evaluating Development Projects*, UNESCO, Second Edition, reprinted, Belgium, 1967, 116 pp.

This is an excellent handbook which incorporates survey methods and other research methods for evaluating social development projects in a variety of countries. The principles discussed are applicable to the formation of social programs in a variety of substantive areas such as agriculture, housing, education, disease control, and so forth.

3. Hess, Irene, Riedel, Donald C., and Fitzpatrick, Thomas B., *Probability Sampling of Hospitals and Patients*, The University of Michigan, Bureau of Hospital Administration, Research series No. 1, 1961.

This monograph discusses principles of probability sampling and their application in selecting representative samples of hospitals and patients. The principles can also be applied to other organizations and social programs.

4. Hyman, Herbert, *Survey Design and Analysis*, The Free Press, Publishers, Glencoe, Illinois, 1957.

Principles and procedures for surveys are presented concisely and logically. Descriptions of actual studies with the questionnaires that were used and principles of data analysis are also included. Chapters One and Two provide the reader with perspectives adopted by the survey analyst and Chapters Eight and Nine are excellent in their discussions of the use of survey findings for public policy and for applied purposes such as programmatic evaluations.

5. Moser, C. A., *Survey Methods in Social Investigation*, Heinemann Educational Books, Ltd., London, 1965.

This is a basic book which covers all aspects of a survey from the definition of the population and sample design to the construction and analysis of questionnaires and interviews.

Case Study

DESCRIPTION

The case-study technique has as its purpose the detailed description of a social program as it unfolds in its process of development. It employs both qualitative and quantitative data in an effort to develop hypotheses and new ideas for explaining the progress or lack of progress in program development. Among the methods used are participant observation, informal interviews, methods of group analysis such as sociometric devices, content analyses of written documents, and so forth.

Experts in this technique are social scientists: the social psychologist for the study of groups; the sociologist for the study of organizations and communities; the anthropologist for the study of cultural and subcultural differences; and the psychologist for the study of individuals. An expert in this technique attempts to accumulate as much information as possible; then he uses that information in relation to a conceptual scheme he develops for generating ideas. For example, a sociologist may be hired to study a social program which includes a group living situation for the purpose of increasing the adjustment of delinquent boys. The expert may seek to participate in the group living situation as an observer, but without responsibility for program operations. He reviews official policies, documents, and rules; and he may live with the group in order to increase his awareness from their perspective. He talks with people connected with the program, and with other organizations that might be closely related to the program. Following this, he may develop a conceptual scheme from his experience in the group and from his previous experiences and knowledge of groups and organizations. Quantitative data are then collected with respect to group behavior and the way in which the program attempts to influence it. That information is used for developing ideas and hypotheses about future program directions, particularly its relation to organizations concerned with delinquency, and its influence on community adjustment through the use of living groups. Moreover, if problems are discovered in the group program, recommendations might be made for their solution.

A detailed case study takes time. However, a small-sized research staff may be sufficient. Thus, the costs involved are primarily those for manpower, possibly tape-recording equipment and other clerical devices, and data processing and report writing. Costs are minimal when case-study experts give a few training sessions to staff in selected methods such as recording procedures and content analysis (see reference below by Riley). The staff, in turn, uses those methods routinely.

USES

Case-study techniques may be particularly useful for developing programs where there is difficulty in specifying objectives and in selecting programmatic means to accomplish those objectives. Furthermore, some of the methods employed in case studies, as indicated above, may be used by program staff. For example, each staff person may keep a diary of what activities he is engaged in, for what reasons, and with what success. Periodically, the content of those diaries is reviewed in order to discover possible strategies that could be used by all staff members more consistently.

The case-study approach can also be used to pinpoint potential problems in program operations. For example, a case study might reveal that the primary problem in not being able to contact program beneficiaries who are representative of the "intended target population" is that there are differences of opinion among staff persons, and between staff and administration, with respect to who should be contacted.

Information from the case study is principally used for an evaluation of program efforts with respect to the nature and quantity of staff activities, and the extent to which staff efforts are related to program goals as perceived by different staff members. However, indirect information can be gathered which bears on possible reasons for program ineffectiveness and inefficiency: location of staff conflicts, different vested interests, and so forth.

REFERENCES

1. Bolgar, Hedda, "The Case Study Method," in *Handbook of Clinical Psychology,*

Ed., Benjamin B. Wolman, McGraw-Hill Book Company, New York, 1965, pp. 28–39.

The nature of the case study approach as used for the discovery and generation of hypotheses in clinical research is discussed.

2. Bloom, Bernard L., "The Evaluation of Primary Prevention Programs," in *Comprehensive Mental Health*, Eds., Leigh M. Roberts, Norman S. Greenfield, and Milton H. Miller, The University of Wisconsin Press, Madison, Wisconsin, 1968, pp. 117–136.

Different types of evaluation are discussed, and guideline questions are presented for mental health program directors. Of particular import is the brief discussion pertaining to the use of a program diary for describing mental health programs.

3. McCall, George J. and Simmons, J. L., Eds., *Issues in Participant Observation*, Addison-Wesley Publishing Company, Reading, Mass., 1969.

This is a book of readings on the method of participant observation. Recommended articles are "Some Methodological Problems of Field Studies" by Morris Zelditch, Jr., pp. 5–18; "Data

Quality Control in Participant Observation," by George J. McCall, pp. 128–141; "Problems of Inference and Proof in Participant Observation," by Howard S. Becker, pp. 245–257; and "A Comparison of Participant Observation and Survey Data," by Arthur J. Vidich and Gilbert Shapiro, pp. 295–302.

4. Riley, Matilda White, *Sociological Research: A Case Approach*, Harcourt, Brace & World, New York, 1963.

This is a text book in research methods for sociologists. The sections on "Descriptive Case Studies," pp. 32–77, "Questioning Compared with Observation," pp. 132–193, and "Uses of Available Data," pp. 194–255 deal with a variety of methods used in case studies: sociometric procedures, observations, interviews, content analysis, and so forth. Advantages and disadvantages of the methods are reviewed in their applications to actual studies.

COST-ANALYTIC TECHNIQUES

Cost Accounting

DESCRIPTION

The purpose of cost-accounting techniques is to relate program costs to program outputs. Outputs are those program actions which are measurable: number of children placed in adoption, number of therapy interviews, number of health examinations, and so forth. The same principles as those in general accounting are used, but in addition, cost accounting produces unit cost figures as a basis for analyzing, budgeting, and allocating resources. The cost accountant is an expert in the use of accounting methods, agency forms, and, often times, in program planning. He reviews general and social accounting records similarly to the auditor. He devises categories of unit costs for program service; then he relates them to the general and social-accounting data, as well as to information from time-and-motion studies, so that he can describe how much money and time are expended for what kinds of staff activities in relation to specified program objectives. For example, statements such as the following might be made: X amount of funds were expended for using Y amount of man-hours to recruit Z number of persons to participate in the social program. Thus, the knowledge from cost accounting is that of simple facts relating program resources to program outputs.

Among the objectives of cost accounting are the improvement of program budgeting and the procurement of information for determining program service priorities as a function of costs. An extension of cost accounting is program budgeting, which organizes cost data for use in assessing alternative program actions in relation to their cost and utility. Program budgeting, which emphasizes program objectives and possible alternatives, is increasingly being employed by the federal government and other large organizations in an attempt to improve program planning within restricted budgets. Pfeiffer (see reference below) gives an excellent introduction to the technique and its possible applications to education.

Cost-accounting and program-budgeting techniques are difficult to employ when the program objectives are unspecified or when the categories of unit cost are ambiguous. Although information relating costs to program outputs can be readily obtained, reliable data relating program objectives to costs and outputs are not easily produced. Thus, the costs for using these techniques increase in relation to the ambiguity and imprecision of program objectives and program outputs related to those objectives. In addition, since cost accounting depends upon an adequate general accounting system, the costs would decrease in relation to the adequacy of the general accounting system used by the program.

USES

Cost-accounting techniques are used primarily for the evaluation of program effectiveness and efficiency in the program-contact stage. For example, a program which intends to give health examinations to a designated population may be evaluated with respect to the relative costs involved in completing examinations in different geographical locations. Moreover, different parts of the examination may be administered by physicians, nurses, non-professionals, etc.; the cost and utility of the use of different professionals for administering different aspects of the program (such as reading an eye chart, weighing the patient, taking a social history, etc.) might be assessed.

The information yielded by cost-accounting studies may be used to initiate different procedures in a social program in relation to general accounting and the redistribution of program efforts. Moreover, cost accounting provides basic data which are used for evaluating the effectiveness and efficiency of social programs by such techniques as cost-benefit analysis, which will be discussed subsequently.

REFERENCES

1. Elkin, Robert, "Analyzing Time, Costs, and Operations in a Voluntary Children's Institution and Agency," Project on Cost

Analysis in Childrens Institutions, North Building, U. S. Department of Health, Education, and Welfare, Washington, D.C., September, 1965, pp. 27–39.

This study employs a variety of cost-accounting procedures as recommended by the Child Welfare League of America.

2. Hill, John G., "Cost Analysis of Social Work Service," in *Social Work Research*, Ed., Norman A. Polansky, The University of Chicago Press, 1960, pp. 223–246.

Principles of cost accounting are discussed for social welfare organizations. They are also applicable to health and education programs.

3. Pfeiffer, John, *New Look at Education*, Odyssey Press, New York, 1968.

In Chapter Two, the author gives an introduction to program budgeting and other methods used for making program decisions.

Cost-Benefit Analysis

DESCRIPTION

Cost-benefit analysis is a technique for evaluating the relative effectiveness of alternative programs, strategies, etc., in terms of cost. Its purpose is to ascertain the relationship of required resources (costs) to the attainment of specified goals (benefits). This type of analysis is geared to answering such questions as which of a number of possible income-maintenance programs will result in optimal benefits under any given allocation of resources (see reference below by Levine). Essential elements in cost-benefit analysis are costs (financial costs of manpower and other resources), benefits (whether or not desired objectives have been achieved, and the monetary value that can be ascribed to such achievements), and the specification of objectives, goals, and values. As is true in cost accounting, program inputs are first related to program outputs or staff actions; program outputs are then related to the results of those actions. The cost-benefit analyst attempts to translate criteria of goal achievement into monetary units, in order to make an appraisal of the economic benefits of the program relative to the costs of program resources and activities. For example, the benefits from a program for training welfare recipients for jobs might be reflected in the extent to which the recipients received jobs, and the amounts of money thus saved from welfare-department expenditures, as well as the amounts of money contributed to society through taxes and so forth. In the comparison of two programs, which, for the sake of illustration, are assumed to be similar in all respects except costs and benefits, that program which has a greater benefit-to-cost ratio would be regarded as the more effective.

Cost-benefit analyses are conducted by economists, systems engineers, and program planners who have developed expertise in the technique. Cost-benefit analysts use accounting methods, economic methods of analysis, along with graphic and tabular presentations to represent mathematical units of relationship. They attempt to convert social indicators of program objectives into economic indices, or into other indices that could be measured and translated into economic terms. Data are gathered from forms for recording program statistics, general and cost-accounting records, social-accountability records, and so forth.

The knowledge produced is in the form of descriptive facts relating costs to benefits. However, such knowledge is valid only insofar as the indicators of "benefits" can be translated into monetary units. Some benefits may not be registerable in monetary equivalents or, just as problematic, the amount of assigned economic value may be purely arbitrary. The costs of such analyses are greater than those for cost accounting because more variables are related. But the potential knowledge derived, when the indicators of "benefits" appear to be accurately reflected in monetary units, is much more useful for making decisions about program alternatives. In fact, a key ingredient in planning is the consideration of alternative uses and amounts of program resources (costs) to achieve specified benefits. Such cost-benefit planning is more likely to lead to efficient alternatives than is cost accounting.

USES

Cost-benefit analyses are employed primarily to evaluate the efficiency and relative effectiveness of social programs that are in the implementation stage of development. As indicated above, analyses are more immediately useful for programs having objectives that can be readily translated into economic units (getting off the welfare roles, receiving jobs at given wages, etc.).

The product of cost-benefit analyses might also contain recommendations for choosing among various alternative strategies for allocating program resources, i.e., a rationale is provided for maintaining or shifting program efforts in relation to costs and benefits.

In the reference below by Levine, a cost-benefit analysis of a government job-retraining program is described. Although benefit/cost ratios were produced with respect to estimated earnings and program costs, psychological and sociological "benefits" were ignored because they could not be easily quantified into monetary units. This deficiency has led different analysts to use a technique which we call cost-outcome analysis. It is discussed in the next section of this chapter.

REFERENCES

1. Alkin, Marvin C., "Evaluating the Cost-Effectiveness of Instructional Programs,"

Center for the Study of Evaluation of Instructional Programs, University of California, Los Angeles, 1969.

Distinctions between cost – benefit analysis and cost-effectiveness evaluation are made, and an approach is presented for evaluating instructional programs in education.

2. Levine, Abraham S., "Cost-Benefit Analysis and Social Welfare: An Exploration of Possible Applications," *Welfare in Review*, Vol. 4, No. 2, February, 1966, pp. 1–11.

Principles of cost-benefit analysis are discussed and applied to social welfare. For illustrative purposes, an actual study of unemployment is presented.

3. Neenan, William B., *Normative Evaluation of a Public Health Program*, Institute of Public Administration, The University of Michigan, 1967, 74 pp.

This is a cost-benefit analysis of the Michigan Department of Public Health's x-ray tuberculosis control program. Economic criteria are presented and applied, and detailed findings of the study are included.

Cost-Outcome Analysis[2]

DESCRIPTION

Cost-outcome analysis is a modification of cost-benefit analysis. Whereas cost-benefit analysis attempts to relate program costs to the results of program activities in terms of monetary units, cost-outcome analysis relates program costs to program results (outcomes) without translating outcomes into economic indicators. The purpose of cost-outcome analysis is to gauge the relative efficiency of the costs of alternative program inputs with respect to the accomplishment of specified objectives. The objectives might be fixed, while the costs of program input vary. For example, the fixed objective might be the attainment of a nondelinquency rate of 90% for a target population of delinquent youth. Two alternative programs with varying costs may both result in a nondelinquency rate of 90%. That program which entails the lower costs would be regarded as the more efficient program. Thus, the essence of cost-outcome analysis is the determination of the minimum costs that are necessary to produce a given outcome.

---

[2] In our review of the literature we found no precise term that could identify this modification of cost-benefit analysis. Therefore, our use of the term, "cost-outcome analysis," is purely arbitrary. Nevertheless, because this is a useful technique in cost analysis we include it along with the other techniques.

Cost-outcome analysis is a technique which involves a combination of social-research and cost-accounting methods. Hence, the expert's background may be similar to that of social researchers (experimentalists or survey analysts) and/or to cost analysts (cost-benefit or cost-accounting analysts).

The knowledge produced is, typically, descriptive facts: group therapy for a designated population is cheaper than individual therapy in achieving a 70% rate of reduction in psychological symptoms; a classroom size of 20 involves less per pupil cost than one of ten for attaining a specified goal of reading improvement; and so forth.

Of course, this technique is most applicable when outcomes can be specified and fixed. When outcomes are variable and costs are also variable, the analysis takes on the character of experimental or survey research, with costs regarded as one of the independent variables that could lead to program results. For example, in the reference below, Alkin discusses a model for cost-effectiveness analysis in instructional programs. He regards student inputs, financial inputs, descriptive characteristics of students and school personnel, and features of external systems in the environment as independent variables which could lead to, or be associated with, program outcomes such as cognitive and noncognitive changes in students.

If program objectives are fixed and easily attained, the technique is not too expensive for comparing the relative costs of different approaches. In such situations, the technique is less costly than cost-benefit analysis, particularly when the criteria for program outcomes are sociological or psychological, as opposed to economic. However, if the technique is expanded to use a variety of program input and outcome measures, the costs would exceed those typically required for surveys and experiments.

USES

Cost-outcome analysis is most useful as a device for assessing the relative efficiency of alternative programs, or aspects of programs, in the implementation stage. However, if outcomes are interpreted broadly to include fixed objectives for achieving specified program goals, then the technique can be employed for all program stages. Answers might be provided to questions such as the following: what are the relative costs for recruiting X number of staff persons, involving Y number of program recipients, delivering Z amounts of services, and so forth.

The technique might also provide information to administrators for making decisions about the distributions of costs that go into program efforts. Moreover, as in Alkin's model, the technique can be used for determining relative efficiency as well as program effectiveness.

REFERENCES

1. Alkin, Marvin C., "Evaluating the Cost-Effectiveness of Instructional Programs," Center for the Study of Evaluation of Instructional Programs, University of California, 1969.

   A model is presented for the use of cost-effectiveness evaluation in instructional programs.

2. Levine, Abraham S., "Evaluating Program Effectiveness and Efficiency: Rationale and Description of Research in Progress," *Welfare in Review*, Vol. 5, No. 2, February, 1967, pp. 1–11.

   A model is formulated for the comparative evaluation of social, educational, and vocational services in AFDC programs.

Operations Research

DESCRIPTION

Operations research, or systems analysis, combines scientific experimentation, mathematics, statistics, and computer technology in an effort to provide data on alternative ways of conducting and coordinating program activities within an organization: assignment of personnel, scheduling, allocation of resources, choosing among alternative programs, and so forth. It may use simultaneously several of the techniques previously described (cost-analytic techniques, social-research techniques, and administrative-audit techniques). Although it has goals which may be similar to those of cost-benefit and cost-outcome analysis, it differs from those techniques in its deliberate use of mathematical models to solve organizational problems. The following ingredients are involved in operations research:

1. The administrative problem is defined. This includes the specification of objectives, the selection of criteria to be employed in measuring those objectives, and the identification of variables that are controllable and uncontrollable (for example, in an education program, *controllable variables* might refer to different programs, different geographical areas where schools could be located, etc.; *uncontrollable variables* might refer to such things as salary regulations for teachers, school enrollment, and so forth).

2. The organizational system of the program is described in an effort to relate program activities to program objectives.

3. A mathematical model is constructed to represent the system and its objectives. For example, "G" might represent a desired proportion of high school graduates as a result of an education program. A

mathematical expression is formulated which relates symbols such as "t," the number of teachers, etc., to "G."

4. A solution is derived mathematically from the model. For example, it might be determined that a certain number of teachers is the minimum number necessary to produce a designated proportion of high school graduates at specified costs.

5. The mathematical model and its solutions, which are abstract representations of the program, are tested. Data are collected in accordance with the model, and the operations researcher determines whether the model fits the actual data.

6. The model and its solutions are revised, if necessary, to fit the data collected from the program.

7. The final solution, as approved by the administrator, is put into program operation.

Operations researchers are drawn from a variety of disciplines, usually engineering, mathematics and statistics, business, and economics. They are expert in the formulation of organizational objectives regarding measurable criteria of effectiveness, the construction and testing of mathematical models, and computer technology. Because operations research involves a great deal of technical knowledge, a team of experts, rather than one individual, is often used. For example, a team may be comprised of a sociologist who is expert in organizational analysis, a mathematician, a computer programmer, and an industrial engineer. In view of the number of experts involved, the use of computers, etc., the cost of using this technique may be relatively greater than that for most other techniques. However, for large-scale programs it may result in the selection of efficient methods which could reduce program costs considerably (see references below for its efficient use in education, business, etc.).

USES

Operations research is employed for programs in the contact and implementation stages of development. It produces information on efficiency and effectiveness, and it provides a basis for making decisions about the distribution of program efforts. It is potentially useful for large-scale programs which need to reduce operating costs, but it may be too costly for small-scale programs with very limited budgets.

Although operations research has had considerable amounts of success in solving military, defense, and business problems, it may not be as applicable as other evaluation techniques for the evaluation of social programs. In particular, this would be the case when *either* the criterion variables are not quantifiable *or* the mathematical expressions do not fit the actual collected data. But its use is promising for dealing with such problems as income distribution for welfare recipients, the delivery of medical services, and so forth.

REFERENCES

1. Hillier, Frederick S. and Lieberman, Gerald J., *Introduction to Operations Research*, Holden-Day, Inc., San Francisco, 1967.

   This is a basic text in operations research. The basic planning involved in operations research is described in the first 20 pages, and this is followed by detailed expositions on probability theory and decision theory, techniques in mathematical programming and techniques in the use of probabilistic models.

2. Pfeiffer, John, *New Look at Education*, Odyssey Press, New York, 1968.

   This book discusses the application of systems analysis to education. Chapter Two on "Decision Making in Action," pp. 16–32, provides a cogent description of the planning involved in systems analysis.

Chapter Five

USE OF CONSULTATION

Throughout this book we have emphasized the key role the program director plays in the planning of social-program evaluations. Thus, we have presented guidelines which can be helpful to the administrator in thinking about differential evaluation. Since program directors are not likely to be expert in conducting most types of evaluations, it is important now to consider ways in which evaluation consultants can be used.

There are at least two phases of evaluation planning in which the administrator may wish to use evaluation consultants. In the first instance, the director may seek consultation to assist in deciding whether or not a program should be evaluated. In considering this question, the program director must take into account dilemmas connected with the potential costs of evaluation, the people and purposes for which the evaluation will be conducted, and the choice of a program evaluator.

With a review of the preceding chapters, and trusting their own competence and knowledge of evaluation techniques, some administrators will be in a position to decide, on their own, whether or not to evaluate. However, evaluation consultants can be of help to many administrators who lack experience and knowledge about evaluation, or who seek to legitimize evaluation efforts. Once the program director has decided to proceed with an evaluation, he is then faced with the task of choosing an evaluator. For this second phase of evaluation planning, there are a number of factors which the administrator needs to consider in selecting an evaluator and in establishing a contract with him.

PROGRAM EVALUATION OR NOT

Administrators are often confronted with the decision of whether or not a program should be evaluated. There are several factors which should be considered in making this decision, and, after the program director's initial examination of these, he may wish to make use of an evaluation consultant. One of the potential advantages in using a consultant is the probability that consultation will provide a clear, informed foundation for later negotiations with an evaluator, in the event that it is decided to carry out an evaluation effort.

The first task of the program director in evaluation

planning is to state with clarity the program's objectives. If the program goals are not specified, then it will be unclear as to what is to be evaluated. Obviously, evaluations cannot provide feedback information regarding the accomplishment of goals when the goals are unknown. Secondly, the degree of certainty of knowledge about the program should be considered. If the director, for example, knows that his program (and programs similar to it) are effective and efficient in achieving program goals, there may be little need for an evaluation. On the other hand, there may be insufficient evidence that the program is working; in fact, the administrator may not even know what activities are specifically taking place in the program. Thirdly, the possibility of change in program goals should be considered. A program which is in the process of development must have feedback information regarding its goals—its successes and failures. Fourthly, one should weigh the relative advantages and disadvantages of evaluation. What kinds of information can be secured from evaluation, and could that information be used for the continuing development of the program?

Previously, we presented the notion of evaluation for different stages of program development as a conceptual device for clarifying the kinds of questions that one would want answered in an evaluation. If one assumes that a program is in one stage of development, and asks questions not appropriate for that stage, the evaluation is not likely to provide information that can be used by program administration. Thus, the process of forming differential evaluation questions is a way of considering whether or not evaluation might be advantageous. Moreover, it is a device for determining the timing of different kinds of evaluation. Evaluations devoted to an assessment of the implementation stage, for example, are not likely to provide useful information to the administrator for making program decisions when his program plan is just being conceived in the program-initiation stage. That is, an evaluation of the implementation stage in this instance would be premature.

The following questions are presented as preliminary guidelines for the administrator who is considering a differential evaluation of a social program:

1. What is the current state of program objectives?
   a. What are current program objectives?
   b. Are the program objectives likely to change?
   c. What is the current state of knowledge of the program?
2. What is the purpose of the evaluation?
   a. What stage of development is to be evaluated?
   b. What are the relative advantages and disadvantages of an evaluation?
   c. Would the program be altered as a result of feedback from the evaluation?

These guidelines point to minimal sets of information necessary for the program administrator's decision on the question of whether or not a program should be evaluated. It is particularly important for the program director to accept major responsibility for ascertaining this information, and he should not expect this task to be performed by an evaluation consultant. However, an evaluation consultant may be of considerable assistance in reviewing the stated objectives of a program, and checking on their clarity and specificity prior to a final decision to evaluate or not.

EVALUATION AT WHAT COST

A major issue which confronts administrators planning evaluation is the cost of an evaluation. What funds are available for an evaluation? What kinds of information can be obtained from evaluations which are limited in their comprehensiveness by the amounts and types of resources that are available? Essentially, the primary question is what are the administrative costs of evaluation in relation to the potential value of an evaluation?

There are two major kinds of costs: primary costs and secondary costs. *Primary costs* are all of the direct costs involved in the procurement of evaluation manpower, time, physical resources, and operational facilities for the conduct of an evaluation. How much money is available to pay evaluation consultants, to provide facilities for the compilation of necessary evaluation data, and so forth? *Secondary costs* are those indirect costs that occur when an evaluation is planned and when it is actually executed. That is, secondary costs are concerned with the effects of the evaluation effort on program operations and the commitments of time, effort, and program resources required to facilitate the evaluation.

A program director should be knowledgeable about the secondary costs as well as the primary costs of evaluation. The reason for this is that program resources used for purposes of an evaluation may detract from the manpower and time necessary for the program staff to carry out its program. While an evaluation is taking place, it is possible that some program costs might be reduced. For example, immediate procedures for the efficient allocation of program resources may be developed. Moreover, it is possible that a program may receive direct financial benefits from an evaluation. This may occur when an evaluation is funded entirely through other sources (e.g., grants for demonstration projects from governmental and private foundations), and part of the evaluation monies are used to subsidize some program costs, such as selected clerical activities.

In summary, the answers to the following questions should be considered by the administrator who is planning an evaluation:

1. What funds from the program and other resources are available for evaluation?
2. What are the primary costs of a proposed evaluation?
3. What are the secondary costs of a projected evaluation?

4. What are the potential benefits of an evaluation?

The extent to which administrators will be able to ascertain the answers to these questions without assistance will depend on several factors, such as the technical competencies of the administrator and staff members, the particular stage of program development, and the kinds of evaluation techniques appropriate to the evaluation. Thus, many administrators will need to use an evaluation consultant when complex evaluation designs, such as experiments, are contemplated at the implementation stage of a program. Evaluation consultants will be of particular help in estimating primary costs of evaluation. The administrator should not hesitate to use an evaluation consultant with regard to cost estimates, for neglect in this area will likely lead to unanticipated conflict, during an evaluation, between the administrator and evaluator. Since costs are so closely interconnected with the choice of evaluation techniques, evaluation consultants competent in the various techniques are ready sources for cost-related planning.

EVALUATION FOR WHOM

In planning for evaluation, the administrator must ask: who is the consumer of evaluation? Different groups who are the consumers of evaluation may have diverse values, and discrepant notions of what the program goals and evaluation should be. For example, a group which has fiduciary responsibility for a program may be most concerned about the potential mismanagement of funds and program efficiency; while a group which is representative of the target population may be most interested in the extent to which the program services are meeting their most pressing community needs. What is an acceptable evaluation for one group of consumers may not be acceptable to another group. In particular, criteria for acceptable evaluations may differ for consumers who have vested interests in the maintenance of a program, as opposed to consumers who are in competition with the program.

In our view, then, it would be unrealistic for an administrator to assume that all consumers of evaluation have equivalent values, and to ignore the socio-political context in which an evaluation might take place. Thus, no single evaluation can serve all consumers in the same way. Even if all groups of potential consumers are known prior to an evaluation, it may be impossible for those groups to agree on program objectives and the criteria for assessing them. Therefore, in the planning of an evaluation, the administrator should consider the following factors:

1. Is the socio-political climate conducive to an evaluation (see Chapter One)?
2. Who are the potential consumers of evaluation?
3. To what groups is the program most accountable; are their priorities regarding program goals and content similar to those of the program staff and administration?

4. Are there other groups which have vested interests in the success of the program, and competing groups with vested interests in the failure of the program?

5. Is there any existing controversy regarding any aspect of the program?

6. To what extent is it possible to solicit the involvement of the above groups in clarifying objectives and criteria for evaluating program goals at different stages of development?

The answers to these questions have implications for the kind of evaluation the program director undertakes, and for the choice of an evaluator. In some sociopolitical contexts, even the carrying out of a survey may be problematic. At the same time, the status and reputation of an evaluator may be sufficiently influential to allow for such an evaluation. Information about the potential consumers of evaluation constitutes an essential part of the discussions between the program director and a prospective program evaluator, as conditions and expectations under which an evaluation can be undertaken are identified.

EVALUATION BY WHOM

Given a decision to evaluate a program, the administrator is concerned with questions such as these: who should conduct the program evaluation; who has the necessary competence; who is available and willing to do an evaluation; and so forth? Perhaps the director's first consideration is whether or not he or one of his staff members can conduct the evaluation, and if so, is outside consultation needed? In this regard, the administrator needs to be alert to the potential advantages and disadvantages in the use of "inside" versus "outside" program evaluators. The traditional argument for the use of an outside evaluator is that he can be more objective, due to a lack of involvement in the organizational system. In addition, the outside evaluator is assumed to be more likely accepted as an expert by the staff and consumers of an evaluation. Since the outside evaluator is not a part of the authority structure of the organization, he is expected to be in a preferred position for giving advice, and for making recommendations which will be less threatening to the administrator and his staff. On the negative side, the outside evaluator is normally unknown to the program staff, and therefore more likely to be a source of anxiety to them and to cause a certain amount of disequilibrium within the organization. Of course, the program director is often able to take steps to minimize these problems through appropriate briefing of staff for the evaluation.

Perhaps the principal advantage of the inside evaluator, who comes from within the organization, is that he is less likely to have entry problems, such as the need to learn about the program objectives and operations, and will be accepted by the staff. The inside evaluator is assumed to have the advantage of knowing the staff, and to be able to carry out an evaluation without upsetting the operations of the program. In addition, it is assumed that the inside evaluator will have values regarding program goals and evaluation objectives which are consistent with those of the administrator. However, the insider's evaluation may be suspect to some, as not being completely objective, and as providing biased findings. Another concern regarding the inside evaluator is that his other organizational roles may present demands which inhibit the conduct of the evaluation and prevent or delay its completion. Finally, while it is generally thought that the inside consultant is less costly than the outside person, this is not necessarily the case, particularly when secondary costs are taken into account.

How does a program director solve this dilemma between the use of inside and outside evaluation consultants and evaluators? By taking our view of differential evaluation, the program director will at times require an outside evaluator, or an inside evaluator, or both. Thus, for some stages of program development, the limitations cited with regard to the use of inside evaluators may be minimal or be easily overcome. At other stages, such as evaluation at the implementation stage of a program, the advantage of an outside evaluator may be most salient. The program director should carefully examine the evaluation needs of the program and seek out evaluators at specific stages of development with inside-outside evaluation issues in mind. If appropriate persons are not available and/or desirable from within the organizational system, the administrator may use an evaluation consultant to assist in selecting an evaluator from outside the system. In some cases, such a consultant will stay on to be the program evaluator, or he may simply assist the administrator in finding an evaluator.

As the program director considers who the evaluator should be, the administrative and technical roles defined for the evaluator must also be taken into account. In general, the evaluator's role may be defined in terms of providing for systematic feedback of information regarding evaluation objectives. In addition, it must be clear whether or not the evaluator is to participate in helping to implement evaluation findings. For example, an administrator may be interested in having an evaluator solve specific problems, obtain specific information, make a report, and depart. Or he may expect the evaluator also to assist in handling possible resistance of staff to evaluation and to change, or to assist in developing skills for solving organizational problems, or to carry out recommendations. In such instances, the program director will seek an evaluator who has certain skills in social relationships and/or training in this area. As the program director defines the evaluator's role, he will then be wise to weigh the relative advantages and disadvantages of evaluators from inside as compared to outside the organization. Thus, when the evaluator's role includes considerable activity in implementing findings directed toward organizational change, the administrator may prefer an inside evaluator.

The administrator must also consider the manner in which an evaluation consultant will be expected to relate to the organization's administrative structure. For example, in some cases the administrator may want to retain complete jurisdiction over his own program staff and the evaluation staff; in other instances, the program director and evaluator may share administrative authority, or work out an agreement of division of responsibility. A characteristic frequently attributed to evaluators is the inability of the administrator to control the behaviors of the evaluation team. This is particularly relevant in the light of the "authoritative" nature of the image of the evaluator. Clearly spelled out administrative relationships become an important prerequisite for sound evaluations, and serve to add predictability to the evaluator's performance. Thus, the role of the evaluator, with appropriate attention to issues regarding inside-outside evaluations, must be carefully thought out as the program director proceeds to select someone to evaluate his program.

Expertise of the Consultant

The selection of an evaluator must, in large part, be based on the expertise required for a particular program evaluation. As we indicated in Chapter Four, most evaluators are not likely to be expert in all evaluation techniques, and different evaluation consultants may differ in their methodological preferences. Thus, one evaluator may emphasize cost-accounting methods, while another may emphasize experimental methods.

In addition to the preference for selected techniques, evaluators may differ in their conceptions of the kinds of knowledge that should be derived from evaluations. Evaluation of a program can be viewed as a field situation in which new insights and hypotheses will be developed for the refinement of theory. Such information might be useful to the evaluator who is a theoretician, but it may not be practicable for the program staff. An alternative conception is that an evaluation can provide facts and verified hypotheses pertinent to the specific program which is being evaluated. In this instance, the evaluator's role may be similar to that of the engineer: he devises and executes an evaluation design to test program hypotheses.

The implication for the administrator who is planning an evaluation is that he should be knowledgeable about what kind of evaluation is desired for what stage of program development. Moreover, the administrator should be aware of the possibility that different evaluators may emphasize divergent values with regard to evaluation.

An evaluator may be in agreement with program goals, and he may view evaluation as a strategy to force the program staff to operate in desired ways. Such an evaluator may be a social reformer who is more interested in program development than in providing information regarding the achievement of program goals. Alternatively, another evaluator may view social programs as essentially wasteful. He may believe that rigorous evaluations usually lead to no significant differences as a result of program efforts, and it is possible that he might sacrifice program substance for inappropriate experimental designs.

An important aspect of the consultant's credentials will be his professional discipline. This partially defines the perspective the individual is likely to take toward evaluation. An important question for the administrator is the extent to which he needs an evaluator who has knowledge of the social practice problems related to the evaluation. Thus, in many cases, maximum benefit comes from an evaluation consultant who is from a discipline other than that of the administrator.

In summary, prior to an evaluation, the administrator should ascertain the specific technical expertise of the prospective evaluator, as well as his conceptual, methodological, and value biases. Then, he should correlate that information with his knowledge of what kind of evaluation is most appropriate to the problem at hand and the potential consumers of the evaluation. The following questions pertaining to the selection of an evaluator are presented as factors that should be considered in planning an evaluation:

1. What is the technical competency of the evaluator?
2. Are technically competent evaluators available?
3. What is the evaluator's conception of evaluation?
4. Does the evaluator have a strong bias in favor of or opposed to the content of the program?

5. Does the evaluator have a vested interest in the program or in competing programs?

The task for the administrator is to select the most pertinent expert for evaluation purposes. Answering the above questions will assist the administrator in making an appropriate selection. Of particular help will be at least an elementary knowledge of techniques of evaluation, such as monitoring techniques, social-research techniques, and cost-analytic techniques. Our review of these techniques in Chapter Four provides a foundation for linking evaluation needs to technical evaluation approaches, and hence, to evaluation experts.

Sources of Evaluation Consultants

There are a number of sources to which the program director may look for evaluation consultants. Within large organizations the program director may turn to other units, such as research, budgeting, statistics, and so forth. In seeking an outside evaluator, the administrator may seek out experts from organizations with programs similar to his, or look to members of professional organizations. A variety of kinds of experts can be found in University settings, and in independent contracting organizations such as survey research centers, private business organizations and consulting firms.

Perhaps the single most relevant contingency regarding the selection of program evaluators is the availability of funds. Since funds are always to some extent limited, the administrator must search for experts within the context of available money. When funds are extremely scarce, the administrator may look to individuals within the organization who have some expertise in evaluation and who can be reassigned to such tasks. Or, under these circumstances, the administrator may search for a consultant (from within or without the organization) who will devote his efforts to seeking funds for evaluation.

While knowledge of these sources is important for finding an appropriate consultant or evaluator, the administrator must also recognize the implications of the expert's organizational ties for the conduct of the evaluation and use of findings. As we have pointed out, when the evaluator comes from within the organization there may be some advantages, such as his more complete knowledge of the program, immediate access to the administrator, minimized entry problems, commitment to evaluation objectives, and so forth. At the same time, particular attention must be given to the administrative arrangements, so that it is clear whether the evaluator's position is advisory to the administrator or subordinate to him. In using evaluators from outside sources, there may be increased objectivity in the evaluation, as well as prestige derived from the status of the individual consultant and/or his organization. Thus, the administrator should be aware of the potential uses and abuses of consultants and evaluators which accrue from the organizational and administrative context in which they are placed.

Exploratory Interviews

At the point where the program administrator has decided upon the need for an evaluation and has located a potential evaluator, he should then proceed to an interview with the individual for an exchange of ideas. As indicated earlier, the administrator has the responsibility for providing the prospective evaluator with information about the program, evaluation objectives, and so forth. This information serves as a principal basis to the administrator and evaluator for deciding whether or not the evaluation can answer questions regarding program objectives, and can be undertaken with available staff and resources.

In our earlier discussion of the expertise of evaluators, we identified several guideline questions to assist the administrator in ascertaining the suitability of an evaluator for a specific evaluation effort. During the exploratory interview, therefore, the administrator is interested in the "goodness of fit" between the evaluator and program objectives, staff, and organizational values. Thus, the administrator wants to learn whether or not the consultant is sensitive to the values of the organization, and the extent to which the consultant's values are congruent with those of the organization. In addition, the administrator wants to discover the evaluator's over-all conception of evaluation, and something about his methodological competence, as well as his understanding of the program to be evaluated. The administrator will want to determine whether or not the evaluator's expertise is relevant to the evaluation task.

During the initial interview(s), the administrator should explore ideas concerning the role relationships of the evaluator to the administration and staff. He will want to make some preliminary assessment of how the evaluator's role will complement the roles of program staff. He should begin to clarify the role of the evaluator, and to formulate ways in which the evaluator will use his own staff and that of the organization to carry out the evaluation. Discussion should also focus on the time period deemed necessary for an evaluation, the amount of time investment required by the evaluator and by the administrator and staff, the costs of employment of the evaluator and his assistants, and the possible use of additional consultants and their relationships to the evaluator.

In the exploratory interviews, the evaluator has the opportunity to learn about the program and evaluation objectives, and to decide whether or not he is interested in the evaluation and wishes to work with the program director. At the same time, the administrator wants to work with someone who is competent, and who can produce information relevant to the program. He therefore makes this assessment during the initial interviews, and determines how well he and the evaluator relate to each other. He seeks out areas which might cause conflict, and which could impede the evaluation efforts, rather than assuming that the evaluation task is solely the responsibility of the evaluator.

ESTABLISHING THE CONTRACT

Perhaps one of the best ways to facilitate the evaluation effort is to establish a contract with the evaluator. The contract should spell out the mutually agreed upon commitments and obligations of the administrator and the evaluator. Included in the contract should be a clear statement of role expectations, commitments of time and personnel, funding commitments, administrative jurisdictions, and proposed use of findings. Since decisions cannot all be made in the planning stage of an evaluation effort, a plan should be made for handling decisions on emerging issues, as well as for the possible renegotiation of the contract at specified dates. An important commitment concerns the type of involvement the administrator and his staff will have in the evaluation process. Both the administrator and the evaluator need a clear understanding in advance of the various alternatives for use of staff, and of the restrictions placed in the evaluator's use of staff. To illustrate, an evaluation consultant might rely on written records and/or the receipt of information from recipients of service, while not using or contacting staff members. Another model might involve the staff member's involvement in data-collection efforts, rating, coding of information, and so forth. In still another model, the staff member may himself be a subject of the evaluation effort, contributing to the evaluation by completing forms, interviews, etc. The essential element here is the specification of the ways in which the evaluator will use and/or study various staff members, so that potential conflicts can be identified and handled. These are particularly important concerns, since they involve staff time and program resources.

Since the purpose of the evaluation is frequently an assessment which will contribute to change and improvement, the role of the evaluator with regard to utilization of findings must be specified. For example, it must be clear whether the evaluator is expected only to make recommendations for change, or also to help bring change about through interpretation of findings, training efforts, and the like.

Based on our review of the various stages of program development, the administrator must negotiate with the evaluator with regard to his relationship to one or more program stages. In some cases, movement from one program stage to another (e.g., program initiation to program contact) will call for a change in program-evaluation expertise. In other cases, there will be advantages in continuing with the same evaluator. The mechanisms for making these decisions should be specified in the initial contract with the evaluator. The administrator will also want to specify times at which he will evaluate the contribution of the evaluator, and when decisions are to be made regarding continuation of employment.

THE EVALUATION PHASE

While the contract between the administrator and the evaluator provides a basis for activities during the evaluation period, there are a number of additional issues which the administrator must resolve. The administrator will want to work with the evaluator to avoid undue resistance to evaluation by staff members, and to create realistic expectations on their part. He will want to be alert to entry problems the evaluator may have, as well as to problems which may come from some staff members becoming over-dependent on the evaluator because he is seen as an oracle or "great authority."

As the evaluation proceeds, the administrator will want to develop further plans with the evaluator for the report of findings; that is, feedback mechanisms which will facilitate the consideration and use of findings. With this in mind, the administrator must attend to the positive aspects of staff involvement and communication regarding the use of evaluation. Although the evaluator is a key person in interpreting the results of an evaluation through reports and personal communication, actual change will likely depend on behaviors of the administrator and staff. The administrator should work with the evaluator throughout the evaluation period, to the extent necessary to reach evaluation objectives and to allow for program change when indicated. The role of the evaluator at the termination phase of an evaluation is of particular concern to the administrator. Under most conditions, the evaluator is not expected to continue with the program indefinitely, and the administrator must anticipate and plan for his departure. Some of the functions performed by the evaluator may well be taken over by the administrator and/or his staff members.

UTILIZATION OF FINDINGS

At the completion of an evaluation, the program director is faced with the task of utilizing the evaluation results for making programmatic decisions. Evaluation consultants can be called upon to assist in answering questions such as the following:

1. What do the findings mean in terms of the program objectives?
2. How can the findings be utilized to bring about changes in a particular program?
3. What implications would the implementation of findings have for the over-all program?
4. What next steps are necessary, such as new evaluation efforts, implementation of change, or movement to new stages of program development?

The program director may want to rely heavily on the

program evaluator for consideration of these questions, or he may wish to include additional consultants in these deliberations. The need for consultation at this point will vary, depending on such factors as the nature of the evaluation objectives, the kinds of knowledge gained from the evaluation, and the type of implementation possible and desirable. Since the evaluation results will deal with the efforts, effectiveness, and efficiency of social programs, the program director will want to consider implementation with regard to information received about these aspects of the program operations. For each of these areas the director will be concerned with the soundness, or validity, of the knowledge obtained, and the extent to which it reduces uncertainty about achievements of program objectives. The evaluator will be a key person in interpreting the meaning of the evaluation findings to the administrator and his staff. In those cases where the administrator must report the evaluation results to outside groups, such as Boards of Directors, it is essential that he capitalize on the expertise of the evaluator, as well as on other available consultants, to assess the implications of the findings.

Following the assessment of the soundness of the evaluation results, the administrator must make decisions regarding what findings can be put into actual program practice. He is concerned here with engineerability of the new knowledge; that is, the extent to which the variables under study are available for control by program personnel, and whether or not the manipulation of the variables is feasible. For example, a variable such as the administrator's control over the budget of his program may have a high degree of manipulability. However, even though highly manipulable, the budget changes would then be evaluated in terms of the strength of their effect on the desired program change, and the feasibility of such activity. Thus, the economic costs of other programs in an organization, and other organizational constraints, would then have to be considered in deciding on whether or not to manipulate the budget.

It is at this point, with the evaluation findings in, that the usefulness of the results must be assessed, and that evaluation efforts take on their full meaning; that is, as a management technique for the administrator of social programs. Evaluation consultants, of course, are key resource persons in regard to the administrator's decisions, but, in the final analysis, the program administrator must take the primary responsibility for the evaluation and the subsequent use of the information. Hence, for the administrator, the evaluation provides a foundation for making decisions about the program based on available, objective information which can be utilized to provide effective and efficient program services in health, education, and welfare.

INDEX

BOOK MANUFACTURE

Social Program Evaluation: Guidelines for Health, Education, and Welfare Administrators was composed, offset printed, and bound by Colonial Press, Inc. Internal design was by the art department of F. E. Peacock Publishers, Inc. Cover design was by Charles Kling & Associates. The type is Caledonia with Lydian display.